The Law of Success in Sixteen Lessons

Volume IV

Napoleon Hill

An Official Publication of the
Napoleon Hill Foundation

The Law of Success in Sixteen Lessons

Volume IV

Published by:

The Napoleon Hill Foundation
P. O. Box 1277
Wise, Virginia USA 24293

Website: www.naphill.org
Email: napoleonhill@uvawise.edu

Napoleon Hill World Learning Center
Purdue University Calumet
2300 173rd Street
Hammond, Indiana 46323
Email: nhf@purduecal.edu

Written by Napoleon Hill

This four-volume set of the Law of Success has been created using the original 1928 edition published by the Ralston University Press, Meriden, Connecticut. No text from the original has been omitted.

The Law of Success in Sixteen Lessons
Volume IV
ISBN 978–1–937641–46–7

TRIBUTES TO "LAW OF SUCCESS"
From Great American Leaders

The publishers feel that you will realize more keenly the enormous value of these lessons if you first read a few tributes from great leaders in finance, science, invention and political Life.

Supreme Court of the United States
Washington, D. C.

MY DEAR MR. HILL: I have now had an opportunity to finish reading your *Law of Success* textbooks, and I wish to express my appreciation of the splendid work you have done in this philosophy. It would be helpful if every politician in the country would assimilate and apply the 16 principles upon which the *Law of Success* is based. It contains some very fine material which every leader in every walk of life should understand.

WILLIAM H. TAFT
(Former President of the United States and Chief Justice).

Laboratory of
Thomas A. Edison

MY DEAR MR. HILL: Allow me to express my appreciation of the compliment you have paid me in sending me the original manuscript of *Law of Success*. I can see you have spent a great deal of time and thought in its preparation. Your philosophy is sound and you are to be congratulated for sticking to your work over so long a period of years. Your students . . . will be amply rewarded for their labor.

THOMAS A. EDISON

PUBLIC LEDGER
Philadelphia

DEAR MR. HILL: Thank you for your *Law of Success*. It is great stuff; I shall finish reading it. I would like to reprint that story "What I Would Do if I Had a Million Dollars" in the Business Section of the Public Ledger.

CYRUS H. K. CURTIS
(Publisher of *Saturday Evening Post, Ladies Home Journal*)

Image reproduction from the introduction to the original 1928 edition.

King of the 5 and 10 Cent Stores

By applying many of the 16 fundamentals of the *Law of Success* philosophy we have built a great chain of successful stores. I presume it would be no exaggeration of fact if I said that the Woolworth Building might properly be called a monument to the soundness of these principles.

F. W. WOOLWORTH

Historic American Labor Leader

Mastery of the *Law of Success* philosophy is the equivalent of an insurance policy against failure.

SAMUEL GOMPERS

A Former President

May I congratulate you on your persistence. Any man who devotes that much time . . . must of necessity make discoveries of great value to others. I am deeply impressed by your interpretation of the "Master Mind" principles which you have so clearly described.

WOODROW WILSON

A Department Store Founder

I know that your 16 fundamentals of success are sound because I have been applying them in my business for more than 30 years.

JOHN WANAMAKER

From the Founder of Kodak

I know that you are doing a world of good with your *Law of Success*. I would not care to set a monetary value on this training because it brings to the student qualities which cannot be measured by money alone.

GEORGE EASTMAN

A Food and Candy Chief

Whatever success I may have attained I owe, entirely, to the application of your 16 fundamental principles of the *Law of Success*. I believe I have the honor of being your first student.

WILLIAM WRIGLEY, JR.

Image reproduction from the introduction to the original 1928 edition.

Publisher's Preface

NAPOLEON HILL'S WORDS have positively influenced millions of people worldwide. His books, lectures, magazine articles, and audio and video programs have shown them the way to personal and professional achievement. So in response to popular demand, and with great pride, the Napoleon Hill Foundation and its Board of Trustees present this edition of Dr. Hill's classic course, *The Law of Success*.

To preserve the integrity of Napoleon Hill's ideas, the text of his first published work is largely unmodified. Our changes have been small. Specifically, *The Law of Success* was originally released in eight volumes; beginning with the third edition, the eight volumes were combined into one facsimile volume. We now present *The Law of Success* in four volumes, newly typeset for modern digital printing processes.

The universal message of *The Law of Success* remains unaltered, however. Because of changes in customs and word use, the language may sometimes appear dated, but the underlying principles are as valid today as they were when Hill first presented them in his dynamic and forceful style. In particular, his use of the masculine gender should be taken to connote "mankind" or "humankind" rather than men alone. No one would have been prouder or more excited by the advances of the women's movement than Dr. Hill, who advocated equal rights and equal opportunity for all people long before it was fashionable.

The Success Philosophy that Napoleon Hill presents in this course and in his other works has withstood the test of time. His principles of success have changed the lives of countless women and men from all walks of life on every continent. They can change your life, too, if you will apply them and get into action.

This power to change your life is the legacy of Napoleon Hill; that is the standard by which all works of motivational literature and programs are measured. To attain your goals and know fulfillment in life, study, think, plan, and apply the principles this book has to offer. To merely read and agree with Dr. Hill is to miss the crucial point of his philosophy: Success comes only when you act on what you know and believe.

What your mind can conceive and believe, you can achieve!

The Napoleon Hill Foundation

CONTENTS

VOLUME I
General Introduction to The Law of Success Course
Lesson 1: The Master Mind
  Your Six Most Dangerous Enemies
Lesson 2: A Definite Chief Aim
  Instructions for Applying the Principles of This Lesson
Lesson 3: Self-Confidence
  Discontentment
Lesson 4: The Habit of Saving

VOLUME II
Lesson 5: Initiative and Leadership
  Intolerance
Lesson 6: Imagination
Lesson 7: Enthusiasm
  The Seven Deadly Horsemen
Lesson 8: Self-Control
  The Evolution of Transportation

VOLUME III
Lesson 9: Habit of Doing More Than Paid For
  The Master Mind
Lesson 10: Pleasing Personality
Lesson 11: Accurate Thought
  Failure
Lesson 12: Concentration

VOLUME IV
Lesson 13: Co-operation   1
  Your Standing Army   40
Lesson 14: Failure   47
Lesson 15: Tolerance   83
Lesson 16: The Golden Rule   109
  Indecision   151

Co-operation

You have failed how many times? How

fortunate! You ought to know, by now,

some of the things NOT *to do.*

You Can Do It If You Believe You Can!

CO-OPERATION IS THE beginning of all organized effort. As was stated in the second lesson of this course, Andrew Carnegie accumulated a gigantic fortune through the co-operative efforts of a small group of men numbering not more than a score.

You, too, can learn how to use this principle.

There are two forms of Co-operation to which your attention will be directed in this lesson; namely:

First, the Co-operation between people who group themselves together or form alliances for the purpose of attaining a given end, under the principles known as the Law of the Master Mind.

Second, the Co-operation between the conscious and the subconscious minds, which forms a reasonable hypothesis of man's ability to contact, communicate with and draw upon *infinite intelligence.*

To one who has not given serious thought to this subject, the foregoing hypothesis may seem unreasonable; but follow the evidence of its soundness, and study the facts upon which the hypothesis is based, and then draw your own conclusions.

Let us begin with a brief review of the physical construction of the body:

"We know that the whole body is traversed by a network of nerves which serve as the channels of communication between the indwelling spiritual ego, which we call mind, and the functions of the external organism.

"*This nervous system is dual.* One system, known as the Sympathetic, is the channel for all those activities which are not consciously directed by our volition, such as the operation of the digestive organs, the repair of the daily wear and tear of the tissues, and the like.

"The other system, known as the Voluntary or Cerebro-spinal system, is the channel through which we receive conscious perception from the physical senses and exercise control over the movements of the body. This system has its center in the brain, while the other has its center in the ganglionic mass at the back of the stomach known as the solar plexus, and sometimes spoken of as the abdominal brain. The cerebro-spinal system is the channel of our volitional or conscious mental action, and the sympathetic system is the channel of that mental action which unconsciously supports the vital functions of the body.

"Thus the cerebro-spinal system is the organ of the conscious mind and the sympathetic is that of the sub-conscious mind.

"But the interaction of conscious and sub-conscious minds requires a similar interaction between the corresponding systems of nerves, and one conspicuous connection by which this is provided is the 'vagus' nerve. This nerve passes out of the cerebral region as a portion of the voluntary system, and through it we control the vocal organs; then it passes onward to the thorax, sending out branches to the heart and lungs; and finally, passing through the diaphragm, it loses the outer coating which distinguishes the nerves of the voluntary system and becomes identified with those of the sympathetic system, *so forming a connecting link* between the two and making the man physically a single entity.

"Similarly different areas of the brain indicate their connection with the objective and subjective activities of the mind respectively, and, speaking in a general way, we may assign the frontal portion of the brain to the former, and the posterior portion to the latter, while the intermediate portion partakes of the character of both.

"The intuitional faculty has its correspondence in the upper area of the brain, situated between the frontal and the posterior portions, and, physiologically speaking, it is here that intuitive ideas find entrance. These, at first, are more or less unformed and generalized in character, but are, nevertheless, perceived by the conscious mind; otherwise, we should not be aware of them at all. Then the effort of Nature is to bring these ideas into more definite and usable shape, so the conscious mind lays hold on them and induces a corresponding vibratory current in the voluntary system of nerves, and this in turn induces a similar current in the involuntary system, *thus handing the idea over to the subjective mind.* The vibratory current which had first descended from the apex of the brain to the frontal brain and thus through the voluntary system to the solar plexus is now reversed and ascends from the solar plexus through the sympathetic system to the posterior brain, this return current indicating the action of the subjective mind."

If we were to remove the surface portion of the apex of the brain we should find immediately below it the shining belt of brain substance called the "corpus callosum." *This is the point of union between the subjective and objective,* and, as the current returns from the solar plexus to this point, it is restored to the objective portion of the brain in a fresh form *which it has acquired by the silent alchemy of the subjective mind.* Thus the conception which was at first only vaguely recognized is restored to the objective mind in a definite and workable form, and then the objective mind, acting through the frontal brain—the area of comparison and analysis—proceeds to work upon a clearly perceived idea and to bring out the potentialities that are latent in it. (From Judge T. Troward, in *The Edinburgh Lectures on Mental Science*.)

The term "subjective mind" is the same as the term "sub-conscious mind," and the term "objective mind" is the same as the term "conscious mind."

Please understand these different terms.

By studying this *dual system* through which the body transmits energy, we discover the exact points at which the two systems are connected, and the manner in which we may transmit a *thought* from the conscious to the sub-conscious mind.

You can not scare a man who is at peace with God, his fellow men and himself. There is no room for fear in such a man's heart. When fear finds a welcome there is something that needs awakening.

This Co-operative *dual nervous system* is the most important form of co-operation known to man; for it is through the aid of this system that the principle of evolution carries on its work of developing *accurate thought,* as described in Lesson Eleven.

When you impress any idea on your sub-conscious mind, through the principle of Auto-suggestion, you do so with the aid of this *dual nervous system:* and when your sub-conscious mind works out a definite plan of any *desire* with which you impress it, the plan is delivered back to your conscious mind through this same *dual nervous system.*

This Co-operative system of nerves literally constitutes a direct line of communication between your ordinary conscious mind and *infinite intelligence.*

Knowing, from my own previous experience as a beginner in the study of this subject, how difficult it is to accept the hypothesis here described, I will illustrate the soundness of the hypothesis in a simple way that you can both understand and demonstrate for yourself.

Before going to sleep at night impress upon your mind the *desire* to arise the next morning at a given hour, say at four A.M., and if your impression is accompanied by a *positive determination* to arise at that hour, your sub-conscious mind will register the impression and awaken you at precisely that time.

Now the question might well be asked:

"If I can impress my sub-conscious mind with the *desire* to arise at a specified time and it will awaken me at that time, why do I not form the habit of impressing it with other and more important *desires?*"

If you will ask yourself this question, *and insist upon an answer,* you will find yourself very near, if not on the pathway that leads to the secret door to *knowledge,* as described in Lesson Eleven.

We will now take up the subject of Co-operation between men who unite, or group themselves together for the purpose of attaining a given end. In the second lesson of this course we referred to this sort of cooperation as *organized effort.*

This course touches some phase of co-operation in practically every lesson. This result was inevitable for the reason that the object of the course is to help the student develop power, and power is developed only through *organized effort.*

We are living in an age of co-operative effort. Nearly all successful businesses are conducted under some form of co-operation. The same is true in the field of industry and finance, as well as in the professional field.

Doctors and lawyers have their alliances for mutual aid and protection in the form of Bar Associations and Medical Associations.

The bankers have both local and national Associations for their mutual aid and advancement.

The retail merchants have their Associations for the same purpose.

The automobile owners have grouped themselves into Clubs and Associations.

The printers have their Associations; the plumbers have theirs and the coal dealers have theirs. Co-operation is the object of all these Associations. The laboring men have their unions and those who supply the working capital and superintend the efforts of laboring men have their alliances, under various flames.

Nations have their co-operative alliances, although they do not appear to have yet discovered the full meaning of "co-operation." The attempt of the late President Wilson to perfect the League of Nations, followed by the efforts of the late President Harding to perfect the same idea under the name of the World Court, indicates the trend of the times in the direction of co-operation.

It is slowly becoming obvious to man that those who most efficiently apply the principle of co-operative effort survive longest, and, that this principle applies from the lowest form of animal life to the highest form of human endeavor.

Mr. Carnegie, and Mr. Rockefeller, and Mr. Ford have taught the business man the value of co-operative effort; that is, they have taught all who cared to observe, the principle through which they accumulated vast fortunes.

Co-operation is the very foundation of all successful leadership. Henry Ford's most tangible asset is the well organized agency force that he has established. This organization not only provides him with an outlet for all the automobiles he can manufacture, but, of greater importance still, it provides him with financial power sufficient to meet any emergency that may arise, a fact which he has already demonstrated on at least one occasion.

As a result of his understanding of the value of the co-operative principle Ford has removed himself from the usual position of dependence upon financial institutions and at the same time provided himself with more commercial power than he can possibly use.

The Federal Reserve Bank System is another example of co-operative effort which practically insures the United States against a money panic.

The chain-store systems constitute another form of commercial co-operation that provides advantage through both the purchasing and the distributing end of the business.

The modern department store, which is the equivalent of a group of small stores operating under one roof, one management and one overhead expense, is another illustration of the advantage of co-operative effort in the commercial field.

In Lesson Fifteen you will observe the possibilities of co-operative effort in its highest form and at the same time you will see the important part that it plays in the development of *power*.

As you have already learned, *power* is *organized effort*. The three most important factors that enter into the process of organizing effort are:

Concentration,
Co-operation and
Co-ordination.

How Power Is Developed Through Co-Operation

As we have already seen, power is organized effort or energy. Personal power is developed by developing, organizing and co-ordinating the faculties of the mind. This may be accomplished by mastering and applying the fifteen major principles upon which this course is founded. The necessary procedure through which these principles may be mastered is thoroughly described in the sixteenth lesson.

The development of personal power is but the first step to be taken in the development of the potential power that is available through the medium of allied effort, or *co-operation*, which may be called group power.

It is a well known fact that all men who have amassed large fortunes have been known as able "organizers." By this is meant that they possessed the ability to enlist the co-operative efforts of other men who supplied talent and ability which they, themselves did not possess.

The chief object of this course is so to unfold the principles of *organized* and *co-operative* or allied effort that the student will comprehend their significance and make them the basis of his philosophy.

Take, as an example, any business or profession that you choose and you will observe, by analysis, that it is limited only by lack of application of *organized* and *co-operative* effort. As an illustration, consider the legal profession.

If a law firm consists of but one type of mind it will be greatly handicapped, even though it may be made up of a dozen able men of this particular type. The complicated legal system calls for a greater variety of talent than any one man could possibly provide.

It is evident, therefore, that mere organized effort is not sufficient to insure outstanding success; the organization must consist of individuals each of whom- supplies some specialized talent which the other members of the organization do not possess.

A well organized law firm would include talent that was specialized in the preparation of cases; men of vision and imagination who understood how to harmonize the law and the evidence of a case under a sound plan. Men who have such ability are not always possessed of the ability to try a case in court; therefore, men who are proficient in court procedure must be available. Carrying the analysis a step further, it will be seen that there are many different classes of cases which call for men of various types of specialized ability in both the preparation and the trial of these cases. A lawyer who had prepared himself as a specialist in corporation law might be wholly unprepared to handle a case in criminal procedure.

In forming a law partnership, the man who understood the principles of *organized, co-operative effort,* would surround himself with talent that was specialized in every branch of law and legal procedure in which he intended to practice. The man who had no conception of the potential power of these principles would probably select his associates by the usual "hit or miss" method, basing his selections more upon personality or acquaintanceship than consideration of the particular type of legal talent that each possessed.

The subject of *organized effort* has been covered in the preceding lessons of this course, but it is again brought up in connection with this lesson for the purpose of indicating the necessity of forming alliances or organizations consisting of individuals who supply *all of the necessary talent that may be needed for the attainment of the object in mind.*

In nearly all commercial undertakings, there is a need for at least three classes of talent; namely, buyers, salesmen and those who are familiar with finance. It will be readily seen that when these three classes of men *organize* and *co-ordinate* their efforts they avail themselves, through this form of *co-operation,* of *power* which no single individual of the group possesses.

Many a business fails because all of the men back of it are salesmen, or financial men or buyers. By nature, the most able salesmen are optimistic, enthusiastic and emotional; while able financial men, as a rule, are unemotional, deliberate and conservative. Both classes are essential to the success of a commercial enterprise; but either class will prove too much of a load for any business, without the modifying influence of the other class.

A good stock of self-confidence and a new suit of clothes will help you land a position without "pull," but remember that nothing will go so far toward helping you hold it as will push, enthusiasm and determination to do more than that for which you are paid.

It is generally conceded that James J. Hill was the most efficient railroad builder that America ever produced; but it is equally well known that he was not a civil engineer, nor a bridge builder, nor a locomotive engineer, nor a mechanical engineer, nor a chemist, although these highly specialized classes of talent are essential in railroad building. Mr. Hill understood the principles of *organized effort* and *co-operation;* therefore, he surrounded himself with men who possessed all this necessary ability which he lacked.

The modern department store is a splendid example of *organized, co-operative effort.*

Each merchandising department is under the management of one who understands the purchasing and marketing of the goods carried in that department.

Back of all these department managers is a general staff consisting of specialists in buying, selling, financing, and the management of units, or groups, of people. This form of *organized effort* places back of each department both *buying* and *selling* power such as that department could not afford if it were separated from the group and had to be operated under its own overhead in a separate location.

The United States of America is one of the richest and most *powerful* nations of the world. Upon analysis, it will be seen that this enormous power has grown gut of the *co-operative* efforts of the states of the Union.

It was for the purpose of saving this power that the immortal Lincoln made up his mind to erase the Mason and Dixon line. The saving of the Union was of far greater concern to him than was the freedom of the slaves of the South. Had this not been so, the present status of the United States as a power among the nations of the world would be far different from what it is.

It was this same principle of *co-operative* effort that Woodrow Wilson had in mind when he created his plan for a League of Nations. He foresaw the need of such a plan as a medium for preventing war between nations; just as Lincoln foresaw it as a medium for harmonizing the efforts of the people of the United States, thereby preserving the Union.

Thus it is seen that the principle of *organized, co-operative* effort through the aid of which the individual may develop personal power, is the selfsame principle that must be employed in developing group power.

Andrew Carnegie easily dominated the steel business during his active connection with that industry, for the reason that he took advantage of the principle of *organized, co-operative* effort by surrounding himself with highly specialized financial men, chemists, sales managers, buyers of raw materials, transportation experts and others whose services were essential to that industry. He organized this group of *"co-operators"* into what he called a "Master Mind."

Any great university affords an excellent example of the necessity of *organized, co-operative* effort. The professorate is made up of men and women of highly specialized, though vastly different, ability. One department is presided over by experts in literature; another department by expert mathematicians; another department by experts in chemistry; another department by experts in economic philosophy; another department by experts in medicine; another, by experts in law, etc. The university, as a whole, is the equivalent of a group of colleges each of which is directed by experts in its own line, whose efficiency is greatly increased through allied or *co-operative* effort that is directed by a single head.

Analyze *power*, no matter where, or in what form, it may be found, and you will find *organization* and *co-operation* as the chief factors back of it. You will find these two principles in evidence in the lowest form of vegetation no less than in the highest form of animal, which is man.

Off the coast of Norway is one of the most famous and irresistible tidal falls in the world. This great whirlpool of ceaseless motion has never been known to give UP any victim who was caught in its rushing embrace of foaming water.

No less sure of destruction are those unfortunate souls who are caught in the great maelstrom of life toward which all who do not understand the principle of *organized, co-operative* effort are traveling. We are living in a world in which the law of the survival of the fittest is everywhere in evidence. Those who are "fit" are those who have *power,* and power is *organized effort.*

Unfortunate is the person who either through ignorance, or because of egotism, imagines that he can sail this sea of life in the frail bark of independence. Such a person will discover that there are maelstroms more dangerous than any mere whirlpool of unfriendly waters. All natural laws and all of Nature's plans are based upon harmonious, *co-operative* effort, as all who have attained high places in the world have discovered.

Wherever people are engaged in unfriendly combat, no matter what may be its nature, or its cause, one may observe the nearness of one of these maelstroms that awaits the combatants.

Success in life cannot be attained except through peaceful, harmonious, *co-operative* effort. Nor can success be attained single-handed or independently. Even though a man live as a hermit in the wilderness, far from all signs of civilization, he is, nevertheless, *dependent* upon forces outside of himself for an existence. The more he becomes a part of civilization the more dependent upon *co-operative* effort he becomes.

Whether a man earns his living by days' work or from the interest on the fortune tune he has amassed, he will earn it with less opposition through friendly *co-operation* with others. Moreover, the man whose philosophy is based upon *co-operation* instead of *competition* will not only acquire the necessities and the luxuries of life with less effort, but he will enjoy an extra reward in *happiness* such as others will never feel.

Fortunes that are acquired through *co-operative* effort inflict no scars upon the hearts of their owners, which is more than can be said of fortunes that are acquired through conflict and competitive methods that border on extortion.

The accumulation of material wealth, whether the object is that of bare existence or luxury, consumes most of the time that we put into this earthly struggle. If we cannot change this materialistic tendency of human nature, we can, at least, change the method of pursuing it by adopting *co-operation* as the basis of the pursuit.

Co-operation offers the two-fold reward of providing one with both the necessities and the luxuries of life and the peace of mind which the covetous never know. The avaricious and covetous person may amass a great fortune in material wealth; there is no denying this fact; but he will have sold his soul for a mess of pottage in the bargain.

Let us keep in mind the fact that all success is based upon power, and power grows out of knowledge, that has been organized and expressed in terms of ACTION.

The world pays for but one kind of knowledge, and that is the kind which is expressed in terms of constructive service. In addressing the graduating class of a business college one of the best known bankers in America said:

> You ought to feel proud of your diplomas, because they are evidence that you have been preparing yourselves for *action* in the great field of business.

> One of the advantages of a business college training is that it prepares you for *action!* Not to belittle other methods of education, but to exalt the modern business college method, I am reminded to say that there are some colleges in which the majority of the students are preparing for practically everything else except *action*.

> You came to this business college with but one object in view, and that object is to learn to render service and earn a living. The latest style of clothing has been of little interest to you because you have been preparing yourself for work in which clothes of the latest style will play no important part. You did not come here to learn how to pour tea at an afternoon party nor to become masters at affecting friendliness while inwardly feeling envy for those who wear finer gowns and drive costly motor cars — you came here to learn how to work!

In the graduating class before which this man spoke were thirteen boys, all of whom were so poor that they had barely enough money with which to pay their way. Some of them were paying their own way by working before and after school hours.

That was twenty-five years ago. Last summer, I met the president of the business college which these boys attended and he gave me the history of each one of them, from the time that they graduated until the time when I talked to him. One of them is the president of one of the big wholesale drug companies, and a wealthy man; one is a successful lawyer; two own large business colleges of their own, one is a professor in the department of economics in one of the largest universities in America; one is the president of one of the large automobile manufacturing companies; two are presidents of banks, and wealthy men; one is the owner of a large department store; one is the vice-president of one of the great railway systems of the country; one is a well established Certified Public Accountant; one is dead; and the thirteenth is compiling this Reading Course on the Law of Success.

Eleven successes out of a class of thirteen boys is not a bad record, thanks to the spirit of *action* developed by that business college training.

> *"Quibbling" over salary "to start with" has lost many a man the big opportunity of a lifetime. If the position you seek is one that you know you can throw your whole heart into, take it, even if you have to work for nothing until you deliver a good sample of your "goods." Thereafter you will receive pay in proportion to the quality and quantity of work you perform.*

It is not the schooling you have had that counts; it is the extent to which you express that which you learned from your schooling through well organized and intelligently directed *action*.

By no means would I belittle higher education, but I would offer hope and encouragement to those who have had no such education, provided they express that which they know, be it ever so little, in intensive *action*, along constructive lines.

One of the greatest Presidents who ever occupied the White House had but little schooling, but he did such a good job of expressing what knowledge he acquired by that little schooling, through properly directed *action*, that his name has been inseparably woven into the history of the United States.

Every city, town and hamlet has its population of those well known characters called "ne'er-do-wells," and if you will analyze these unfortunate people, you will observe that one of their outstanding features is *procrastination*.

Lack of *action* has caused them to slip backward until they got into a "rut," where they will remain unless, through accident, they are forced out into the open road of struggle where unusual *action* will become necessary.

Don't let yourself get into such a condition.

Every office, and every shop, and every bank, and every store, and every other place of employment has its outstanding victims of *procrastination* who are doing the goose-step down the dusty road of *failure* because they have not developed the habit of expressing themselves in *action*.

You can pick out these unfortunates all about you if you will begin to analyze those with whom you come in contact each day. If you will talk to them you will observe that they have built up a false philosophy somewhat of this nature:

"I am doing all I am paid to do, and I am getting by."

Yes, they are "getting by"—but that is all they are getting.

Some years ago, at a time when labor was scarce and wages unusually high, I observed scores of able-bodied men lying about in the parks of Chicago, doing nothing. I became curious to know what sort of an alibi they would offer for their conduct, so I went out one afternoon and interviewed seven of them.

With the aid of a generous supply of cigars and cigarettes and a little loose change I bought myself into the confidence of those whom I interviewed and thereby gained a rather intimate view of their philosophy. All gave exactly the same reason for being there, without employment. They said: "The world will not give me a chance!!!"

The exclamation points are my own.

Think of it—the world would not "give them a chance."

Of course the world wouldn't *give* them a chance.

It never *gives* anyone a chance. A man who wants a chance may create it through *action,* but if he waits for someone to hand it to him on a silver platter he will meet with disappointment.

I fear that this excuse that the world does not give a man a chance is quite prevalent, and I strongly suspect that it is one of the commonest causes of poverty and failure.

The seventh man that I interviewed on that well-spent afternoon was an unusually fine looking specimen, physically. He was lying on the ground asleep, with a newspaper over his face. When I lifted the paper from his face, he reached up, took it out of my hands, put it back over his face and went right on sleeping.

Then I used a little strategy by removing the paper from his face and placing it behind me, where he could not get it. He then sat up on the ground and I interviewed him. That fellow was a graduate from two of the great universities of the east, with a master's degree from one, and a Ph.D. from the other.

His story was pathetic.

He had held job after job, but always his employer or his fellow employee "had it in for him." He hadn't been able to make them see the value of his college training. They wouldn't "give him a chance."

Here was a man who might have been at the head of some great business, or the outstanding figure in one of the professions had he not built his house upon the sands of *procrastination* and held to the false belief that the world should pay him for *what he knew!*

Luckily, most college graduates do not build upon such flimsy foundations, because no college on earth can crown with success the man who tries to collect for that which he knows instead of that which he *can do with what he knows.*

The man to whom I have referred was from one of the best known families of Virginia. He traced his ancestry back to the landing of the Mayflower. He threw back his shoulders, pounded himself on the breast with his fist and said: "Just think of it, sir! I am a son of one of the first families of old Virginia!"

My observations lead me to believe that being the son of a "first family" is not always fortunate for either the son or the family. Too often these sons of "first families" try to slide home from third base on their family names. This may be only a peculiar notion of mine, but I have observed that the men and women who are doing the world's work have but little time, and less inclination, to brag about their ancestry.

Not long ago I took a trip back to southwest Virginia, where I was born. It was the first time I had been there in over twenty years. It was a sad sight to compare the sons of some of those who were known as "first families" twenty years ago, with the sons of those who were but plain men who made it their business to express themselves in *action* of the most intensive nature.

The comparison reflected no credit upon the "first family" boys! It is with no feeling of exaltation that I express my gratitude for not having been brought into the world by parents who belonged to the "first family" class. That, of course, was not a matter of choice with me, and if it had been perhaps I, too, would have selected parents of the "first family" type.

Not long ago I was invited to deliver an address in Boston, Mass. After my work was finished, a reception committee volunteered to show me the sights of the city, including a trip to Cambridge, where we visited Harvard University. While there, I observed many sons of "first families"—some of whom were equipped with Packards.

Here's a good joke to play on your employer: Get to your work a little earlier and leave a little later than you are supposed to. Handle his tools as if they belonged to you. Go out of your way to say a kind word about him to your fellow-workers. When there is extra work that needs to be done, volunteer to do it. Do not show surprise when he "gets on to you" and offers you the head of the department or a partnership in the business, for this is the best part of the "joke."

Twenty years ago I would have felt proud to be a student at Harvard, with a Packard car, but the illuminating effect of my more mature years has led me to the conclusion that had I had the privilege of going to Harvard I might have done just as well without the aid of a Packard.

I noticed some Harvard boys who had no Packards. They were working as waiters in a restaurant where I ate, and as far as I could see they were missing nothing of value because they owned no Packards; nor did they seem to be suffering by comparison with those who could boast of the ownership of parents of the "first family" type.

All of which is no reflection upon Harvard University—one of the great universities of the world—nor upon the "first families" who send boys to Harvard. To the contrary, it is intended as a bit of encouragement to those unfortunates who, like myself, have but little and know but little, but express what little they know in terms of constructive, useful *action*.

The psychology of *inaction* is one of the chief reasons why some towns and cities are dying with the dry-rot!

Take the city of X, for example. You'll recognize the city by its description, if you are familiar with this part of the country. Sunday blue-laws have closed up all the restaurants on Sunday. Railroad trains must slow down to twelve miles an hour while passing through the city. "Keep off the grass" signs are prominently displayed in the parks. Unfavorable city ordinances of one sort or another have driven the best industries to other cities. On every hand one may see evidence of restraint. The people of the streets show signs of restraint in their faces, and in their manner, and in their walk.

The mass psychology of the city is negative.

The moment one gets off the train at the depot, this negative atmosphere becomes depressingly obvious and makes one want to take the next train out again. The place reminds one of a grave-yard and the people resemble walking ghosts.

They register no signs of *action!*

The bank statements of the banking institutions reflect this nega-tive, *inactive* state of mind. The stores reflect it in their show windows and in the faces of their salespeople. I went into one of the stores to buy a pair of hose. A young woman with bobbed hair who would have been a "flapper" if she hadn't been too lazy, threw out a box of hose on the counter. When I picked up the box, looked the hose over and registered a look of disapproval on my face, she languidly yawned:

"They're the best you can get in this dump!"

"Dump!" She must have been a mind reader, for "dump" was the word that was in my mind before she spoke. The store reminded me of a rubbish dump; the city reminded me of the same. I felt the stuff getting into my own blood. The negative psychology of the people was actually reaching out and gathering me in.

Maine is not the only state that is afflicted with a city such as the one I have described. I could name others, but I might wish to go into politics some day; therefore, I will leave it to you to do your own analyzing and comparing of cities that are alive with *action* and those that are slowly dying with the dry-rot of *inaction.*

I know of some business concerns that are in this same state of *inaction,* but I will omit their names. You probably know some, too.

Many years ago Frank A. Vanderlip, who is one of the best known and most capable bankers in America, went to work for the National City Bank, of New York City.

His salary was above the average from the start, for the reason that he was capable and had a record of successful achievement that made him a valuable man.

He was assigned to a private office that was equipped with a fine mahogany desk and an easy chair. On the top of the desk was an electric push button that led to a secretary's desk outside.

The first day went by without any work coming to his desk. The second, and third, and fourth days went by without any work. No one came in or said anything to him.

By the end of the week he began to feel uneasy (Men of *action* always feel uneasy when there is no work in sight.)

The following week Mr. Vanderlip went into the president's office and said, "Look here, you are paying me a big salary and giving me nothing to do and it is grating on my nerves!"

The president looked up with a lively twinkle in his keen eyes.

"Now I have been thinking," Mr. Vanderlip continued, "while sitting in there with nothing to do, of a plan for increasing the business of this bank."

The president assured him that both "thinking" and "plans" were valuable, and asked him to continue with his interview.

"I have thought of a plan," Mr. Vanderlip went on, "that will give the bank the benefit of my experience in the bond business. I propose to create a bond department for this bank and advertise it as a feature of our business."

"What! this bank advertise?" queried the president. "Why, we have never advertised since we began business. We have managed to get along without it."

"Well, this is where you are going to begin advertising," said Mr. Vanderlip, "and the first thing you are going to advertise is this new bond department that I have planned."

Mr. Vanderlip won! Men of *action* usually win—that is one of their distinctive features. The National City Bank also won, because that interview was the beginning of one of the most progressive and profitable advertising campaigns ever carried on by any bank, with the result that the National City Bank became one of the most powerful financial institutions of America.

There were other results, also, that are worth naming. Among them the result that Mr. Vanderlip grew with the bank, as men of *action* usually grow in whatever they help to build, until finally he became the president of that great banking house.

In the lesson on *Imagination* you learned how to recombine old ideas into new plans, but no matter how practical your plans may be they will be useless if they are not expressed in *action*. To dream dreams and see visions of the person you would like to be or the station in life you would like to obtain are admirable provided you transform your dreams and visions into reality through intensive *action*.

There are men who dream, but do nothing more. There are others who take the visions of the dreamers and translate them into stone, and marble, and music, and good books, and railroads, and steamships. There are still others who *both dream* and transform these dreams into reality. They are the dreamer-doer types.

There is a psychological as well as an economic reason why you should form the habit of intensive *action*. Your body is made up of billions of tiny cells that are highly sensitive and amenable to the influence of your mind. If your mind is of the lethargic, *inactive* type, the cells of your body become lazy and inactive also. Just as the stagnant water of an inactive pond becomes impure and unhealthful, so will the cells of an inactive body become diseased.

Laziness is nothing but the influence of an inactive mind on the cells of the body. If you doubt this, the next time you feel lazy take a Turkish bath and have yourself well rubbed down, thereby stimulating the cells of your body by artificial means, and see how quickly your laziness disappears. Or, a better way than this turn your mind toward some game of which you are fond and notice how quickly the cells of your body will respond to your enthusiasm and your lazy feeling will disappear.

The cells of the body respond to the state of mind in exactly the same manner that the people of a city respond to the mass psychology that dominates the city. If a group of leaders engage in sufficient *action* to give a city the reputation of being a "live-wire" city this *action* influences all who live there. The same principle applies to the relationship between the mind and the body. An *active,* dynamic mind keeps the cells of which the physical portions of the body consist, in a constant state of activity.

The artificial conditions under which most inhabitants of our cities live have led to a physical condition known as auto-intoxication, which means self-poisoning through the inactive state of the intestines. Most headaches may be cured in an hour's time by simply cleansing the lower intestines with an enema.

Eight glasses of water a day and a reasonable amount of physical *action* popularly known as "exercise" will take the place of the enema. Try it for a week and then you will not have to be urged to keep it up, for you will feel like a new person, unless the nature of your work is such that you get plenty of physical exercise and drink plenty of water in the regular course of your duties.

On two pages of this book enough sound advice could be recorded to keep the average person healthy and ready for *action* during sixteen of the twenty-four hours of the day, but the advice would be so simple that most people would not follow it.

The amount of work that I perform every day and still keep in good physical condition is a source of wonderment and mystery to those who know me intimately, yet there is no mystery to it, and the system I follow does not cost anything.

Here it is, for your use if you want it:

FIRST: I drink a cup of hot water when I first get up in the morning, before I have breakfast.

Second: My breakfast consists of rolls made of whole wheat and bran, breakfast cereal, fruit, soft-boiled eggs once in a while, and coffee. For luncheon I eat vegetables (most any kind), whole wheat bread and a glass of buttermilk. Supper, a well cooked steak once or twice a week, vegetables, especially lettuce, and coffee.

Third: I walk an average of ten miles a day: five miles into the country and five miles back, using this period for meditation and thought. Perhaps the thinking is as valuable, as a health builder, as the walk.

Fourth: I lie across a straight bottom chair, flat on my back, with most of my weight resting on the small of my back, with my head and arms relaxed completely, until they almost touch the floor. This gives the nervous energy of my body an opportunity to balance properly and distribute itself, and ten minutes in this position will completely relieve all signs of fatigue, no matter how tired I may be.

Fifth: I take an enema at least once every ten days, and more often if I feel the need of it, using water that is a little below blood temperature, with a tablespoonful of salt in it, chest and knee position.

Sixth: I take a hot shower bath, followed immediately by a cold shower, every day, usually in the morning when I first get up.

These simple things I do for myself. Mother Nature attends to everything else necessary for my health.

> *Every failure will teach you a lesson that you need to learn if you will keep your eyes and ears open and be willing to be taught. Every adversity is usually a blessing in disguise. Without reverses and temporary defeat, you would never know the sort of metal of which you are made.*

I cannot lay too much stress upon the importance of keeping the intestines clean, for it is a well known fact that the city dwellers of today ire literally poisoning themselves to death by neglecting to cleanse their intestines with water. You should not wait until you are constipated to take an enema. When you get to the stage of constipation you are practically ill and immediate relief is absolutely essential, but if you will give yourself the proper attention regularly, just as you attend to keeping the outside of your body clean, you will never be bothered with the many troubles which constipation brings.

For more than fifteen years no single week ever passed without my having a headache. Usually I administered a dose of aspirin and got temporary relief. I was suffering with auto-intoxication and did not know it, for the reason that I was not constipated.

When I found out what my trouble was I did two things, both of which I recommend to you; namely, *I quit using aspirin* and I cut down my daily consumption of food nearly one half.

Just a word about aspirin — a word which those who profit by its sale will not like — it affords no permanent cure of headache. All it does might be compared to a lineman that cuts the telegraph wire while the operator is using that wire in a call for aid from the fire department to save the burning building in which he is located. Aspirin cuts or "deadens" the line of nerve communication that runs from the stomach or the intestinal region, where auto-intoxication is pouring poison into the blood, to the brain, where the effect of that poison is registering its call in the form of intense pain.

Cutting the telegraph line over which a call for the fire department is being sent does not put out the fire; nor does it remove the cause to deaden, with the aid of a dose of aspirin, the nerve line over which a headache is registering a call for help.

You cannot be a person of *action* if you permit yourself to go without proper physical attention until autointoxication takes your brain and kneads it into an inoperative mass that resembles a ball of putty. Neither can you be a person of *action* if you eat the usual devitalized concoction called "white bread" (which has had all the real food value removed from it) and twice as much meat as your system can digest and properly dispose of.

You cannot be a person of *action* if you run to the pill bottle every time you have, or *imagine* you have, an ache or a pain, or swallow an aspirin tablet every time your intestines call on your brain for a douche bag of water and a spoonful of salt for cleansing purposes.

You cannot be a person of *action* if you *overeat* and *under-exercise*.

You cannot be a person of *action* if you read the patent medicine booklets and begin to imagine yourself ailing with the symptoms described by the clever advertisement writer who has reached your pocket book through the power of *suggestion*.

I have not touched a drug for more than five years, and I have not been either sick or ailing during that time, in spite of the fact that I perform more work each day than most men of my profession. I have *enthusiasm, endurance* and *action* because I eat the sort of simple food that contains the body-building elements that I require, and look after the eliminative processes as carefully as I bathe my body.

If these simple and frank admissions appeal to you as being based upon common sense, take them and put them to the test, and if they serve you as well as they are serving me, both of us will have profited by the courage I had to summon to list them as a part of this lesson.

Usually, when anyone except a physician offers suggestions on the care of the body, he is immediately catalogued as a "long-haired crank," and I will admit that the analysis is often correct. In this instance, I make no stronger recommendations than this:

That you try an enema the next time you have a headache, and if any of the other suggestions appeal to you give them a trial until you are satisfied that they are either sound or unsound.

Before leaving the subject, perhaps I should explain that water which is barely luke-warm should be used for the enema for the reason that this causes the muscles of the intestines to contract, which, in turn, forces the poisonous matter out of the pores of the mucous linings. This exercises those muscles and eventually, it will so develop them that they will do their work in the natural way, without the aid of the enema. A warm water enema is very detrimental for the reason that it relaxes the muscles of the intestines, which, in time, causes them to cease functioning altogether, producing what is ordinarily referred to as the "enema habit."

With due apologies to my friends, the physicians and osteopaths and chiropractors and other health builders, I will now invite you back to that part of the subject of this lesson over which there can be no conflict of opinion as to the soundness of my counsel.

There is another enemy which you must conquer before you can become a person of *action,* and that is the *worry habit.*

Worry, and envy, and jealousy, and hatred, and doubt, and fear are all states of mind which are fatal to *action.*

Any of these states of mind will interfere with, and in some instances destroy altogether, the digestive process through which the food is assimilated and prepared for distribution through the body. This interference is purely physical, but the damage does not stop here, because these negative states of mind destroy the most essential factor in the achievement of *success;* namely, *desire* to achieve.

In the second lesson of this course you learned that your *definite chief aim* in life should be supported by a *burning desire* for its realization. You can have no *burning desire* for achievement when you are in a negative state of mind, no matter what the cause of that state of mind may be.

To keep myself in a positive frame of mind I have discovered a very effective "gloom-chaser." That may not be a very dignified way of expressing my meaning, but since the subject of this lesson is *action* and not dignity I will make it serve. The "gloom-chaser" to which I refer is a hearty laugh. When I feel "out of sorts" or inclined to argue with somebody over something that is not worthy of discussion, I know that I need my "gloom-chaser," and I proceed to get away where I will disturb no one and have a good hearty laugh. If I can find nothing really funny about which to laugh I simply have a forced laugh. The effect is the same in both cases.

Five minutes of this sort of mental and physical exercise—for it is both—will stimulate *action* that is free from negative tendencies.

Do not take my word for this—try it!

Not long ago I heard a phonograph record entitled, as I recall it, *The Laughing Fool,* which should be available to all whose dignity forbids them to indulge in a hearty laugh for their health's sake. This record was all that its name implies. It was made by a man and a woman; the man was trying to play a cornet and the woman was laughing at him. She laughed so effectively that she finally made the man laugh, and the suggestion was so pronounced that all who heard it usually joined in and had a good laugh, whether they felt like it or not.

"As a man thinketh in his heart, so is he."

You cannot think *fear* and act courageously. You cannot think hatred and act in a kindly manner toward those with whom you associate. The dominating thoughts of your mind—meaning by this, the strongest and deepest and most frequent of your thoughts—influence the physical *action* of your body.

An occasional misfortune is a good thing. It reminds us that no one has absolute independence.

Every thought put into action by your brain reaches and influences every cell in your body. When you think *fear* your mind telegraphs this thought down to the cells that form the muscles of your legs and tells those muscles to get into *action* and carry you away as rapidly as they can. A man who is afraid runs away because his legs carry him, and they carry him because the *fear* thought in his mind instructed them to do so, even though the instructions were given unconsciously.

In the first lesson of this course you learned how *thought* travels from one mind to another, through the principle of telepathy. In this lesson you should go a step further and learn that *your thoughts* not only register themselves in the minds of other people, through the principle of telepathy, but, *what is a million times more important to you to understand, they register themselves on the cells of your own body and affect those cells in a manner that harmonizes with the nature of the thoughts.*

To understand this principle is to understand the soundness of the statement: "As a man thinketh in his heart, so is he."

Action, in the sense that the term is used in this lesson, is of two forms. One is physical and the other is mental. You can be very active with your mind while your body is entirely inactive, except as to the involuntary action of the vital organs. Or you can be very active with both body and mind.

In speaking of men of *action,* either or both of two types may be referred to. One is the care-taker type and the other is the promoter or salesman type. Both of these types are essential in modern business, industry and finance. One is known as a "dynamo'" while the other is often referred to as a "balance wheel."

Once in a great while you will find a man who is both a dynamo and a balance wheel, but such well balanced personalities are rare. Most successful business organizations that assume great size are made up of both of these types.

The "balance wheel" who does nothing but compile facts and figures and statistics is just as much a man of *action* as the man who goes upon the platform and sells an idea to a thousand people by the sheer power of his *active* personality. To determine whether a man is a man of *action* or not it is necessary to analyze both his mental and his physical habits.

In the first part of this lesson I said that "the world pays you for what you do and not for what you know." That statement might easily be misconstrued. What the world really pays you for is *what you do* or *what you can get others to do.*

A man who can induce others to co-operate and do effective team-work, or inspire others so that they become more *active,* is no less a man of *action* than the man who renders effective service in a more direct manner.

In the field of industry and business there are men who have the ability so to inspire and direct the efforts of others that all under their direction accomplish more than they could without this directing influence. It is a well known fact that Carnegie so ably directed the efforts of those who constituted his personal staff that he made many wealthy men of those who would never have become wealthy without the directing genius of his brain. The same may be said of practically all great leaders in the field of industry and business — the gain is not all on the side of the leaders. Those under their direction often profit most by their leadership.

It is a common practice for a certain type of man to berate his employers because of their opposite stations in a financial sense. It is usually true that such men would be infinitely worse off without these employers than they are with them.

In the first lesson of this course the value of allied effort was particularly emphasized for the reason that some men have the vision to plan while others have the ability to carry plans into *action* although they do not possess the *imagination* or the vision to create the plans they execute.

It was his understanding of this principle of allied effort that enabled Andrew Carnegie to surround himself with a group of men that was made up of those who could plan and those who could execute. Carnegie had in his group of assistants some of the most efficient salesmen in the world, but if his entire staff had been made up of men who could do nothing but sell he could never have accumulated the fortune that he did. If his entire staff had been made up of salesmen only he would have had *action* in abundance, but *action,* in the sense that it is used in this lesson, must be intelligently guided.

One of the best known law firms in America is made up of two lawyers, one of whom never appears in court. He prepares the firm's cases for trial and the other member of the firm goes to court and tries them. Both are men of intense *action,* but they express it in different ways.

There can be as much *action* in *preparation,* in most undertakings, as in *execution.*

In finding your own place in the world, you should analyze yourself and find out whether you are a "dynamo" or a "balance wheel," and select a *definite chief aim* for yourself that harmonizes with your native ability. If you are in business with others, you should analyze them as well as yourself, and endeavor to see that each person takes the part for which his temperament and native ability best fit him.

Stating it another way, people may be classified under two headings: one is the promoter and the other is the care-taker. The promoter type makes an able salesman and organizer. The care-taker type makes an excellent conserver of assets after they have been accumulated.

Place the care-taker type in charge of a set of books and he is happy, but place him on the outside selling and he is unhappy and will be a failure at his job. Place the promoter in charge of a set of books and he will be miserable. His nature demands more intense *action.* Action of the passive type will not satisfy his ambitions, and if he is kept at work which does not give him the action his nature demands he will be a failure. It very frequently turns out that men who embezzle funds in their charge are of the promoter type and they would not have yielded to temptation had their efforts been confined to the work for which they are best fitted.

Give a man the sort of work that harmonizes with his nature and the best there is in him will exert itself. One of the outstanding tragedies of the world is the fact that most people never engage in the work for which they are best fitted by nature.

Too often the mistake is made, in the selection of a life-work, of engaging in the work which seems to be the most profitable from a monetary viewpoint, without consideration of native ability. If money alone brought *success* this procedure would be all right, but success in its highest and noblest form calls for peace of mind and enjoyment and happiness which come only to the man who has found the work that he likes best.

The main purpose of this course is to help you analyze yourself and determine what your native ability best fits you to do. You should make this analysis by carefully studying the chart that accompanies the Introductory Lesson before you select your *definite chief aim*.

We come, now, to the discussion of the principle through which *action* may be developed. To understand how to become *active* requires understanding of how not to *procrastinate*.

These suggestions will give you the necessary instructions:

FIRST: Form the *habit* of doing each day the most distasteful tasks first. This procedure will be difficult at first, but after you have formed the *habit* you will take pride in pitching into the hardest and most undesirable part of your work first.

SECOND: Place this sign in front of you where you can see it in your daily work, and put a copy in your bedroom, where it will greet you as you retire and when you arise: *"Do not tell them what you can do; show them!"*

THIRD: Repeat the following words, aloud, twelve times each night just before you go to sleep: "Tomorrow I will do everything that should be done, when it should be done, and as it should be done. I

> *Thousands of people walked over the great Calumet Copper Mine without discovering it. Just one lone man got busy with a pick and found it. You may be standing on your "Calumet Mine" right now, without knowing it, in whatever position you are filling. Dig down and see what is under the surface of your position.*

will perform the most difficult tasks first because this will destroy the habit of procrastination and develop the habit of *action* in its place."

FOURTH: Carry out these instructions with faith in their soundness and with belief that they will develop *action,* in body and in mind, sufficient to enable you to realize your *definite chief aim.*

The outstanding feature of this course is the simplicity of the style in which it is written. All great fundamental truths are simple, in final analysis, and whether one is delivering an address or writing a course of instruction, the purpose should be to convey impressions and statements of fact in the clearest and most concise manner possible.

Before closing this lesson, permit me to go back to what was said about the value of a hearty laugh as a healthful stimulant to *action* and add the statement that singing produces the same effect, and in some instances is far preferable to laughing.

Billy Sunday is one of the most dynamic and *active* preachers in the world, yet it has been said that his sermons would lose much of their effectiveness if it were not for the psychological effect of his song services.

It is a well known fact that the German army was a winning army at the beginning, and long after the beginning of the world war; and it has been said that much of this was due to the fact that the German army was a singing army. Then came the khaki-clad doughboys from America, and they, too, were singers. Back of their singing was an enduring faith in the cause for which they were fighting. Soon the Germans began to quit singing, and as they did so the tide of war began to turn against them.

If church attendance had nothing else to recommend it, except the psychological effect of the song service, that would be sufficient, for no one can join in the singing of a beautiful hymn without feeling better for it.

For many years I have observed that I could write more effectively after having participated in a song service. Prove my statement to your own satisfaction by going to church next Sunday morning and participating in the song service with all the enthusiasm at your command.

During the war I helped devise ways and means of speeding production in industrial plants that were engaged in manufacturing war supplies. By actual test, in a plant employing 3,000 men and women, the production was increased forty-five per cent in less than thirty days after we had organized the workers into singing groups and installed orchestras and bands that played at ten-minute intervals such stirring songs as "Over There," and "Dixie," and "There'll Be a Hot Time in the Old Town Tonight." The workers caught the rhythm of the music and speeded up their work accordingly.

Properly selected music would stimulate any class of workers to greater *action,* a fact which does not seem to be understood by all who direct the efforts of large numbers of people.

In all my travels I have found but one business firm whose managers made use of music as a stimulant for their workers. This was the Filene Department Store, in Boston, Mass. During the summer months this store provides an orchestra that plays the latest dance music for half an hour before opening time, in the morning. The salespeople use the aisles of the store for dancing and by the time the doors are thrown open they are in an *active* state of mind and body that carries them through the entire day.

Incidentally, I have never seen more courteous or efficient salespeople than those employed by the Filene store. One of the department managers told me that every person in his department performed more service and with less real effort, as a result of the morning music program.

A singing army is a winning army, whether on the field of battle, in warfare, or behind the counters in a department store. There is a book entitled *Singing Through Life With God* by George Wharton James, which I recommend to all who are interested in the psychology of song.

If I were the manager of an industrial plant in which the work was heavy and monotonous, I would install some sort of musical program that would supply every worker with music. On lower Broadway, in New York City, an ingenious Greek has discovered how to entertain his customers and at the same time speed up the work of his helpers by the use of a phonograph. Every boy in the place keeps time with the music as he draws the cloth across the shoes, and seems to get considerable fun out of his work in doing so. To speed up the work the proprietor has but to speed up the phonograph.

Any form of group effort, where two or more people form a co-operative alliance for the purpose of accomplishing a definite purpose, becomes more powerful than mere individual effort.

A football team may win consistently and continuously, by well co-ordinated team-work, even though the members of the team may be unfriendly and out of harmony in many ways outside of their actual work on the ball ground.

A group of men composing a board of directors may disagree with one another; they may be unfriendly, and in no way in sympathy with one another, and still carry on a business which appears to be very successful.

A man and his wife may live together, accumulate a fair sized or even a great fortune, rear and educate a family, without the bond of harmony which is essential for the development of a Master Mind.

But all of these alliances might be made more powerful and effective if based upon a foundation of perfect harmony, thus permitting the development of a supplemental power known as the Master Mind.

Plain co-operative effort produces power; there can be no doubt about this; but co-operative effort that is based upon complete harmony of purpose develops super-power.

Let every member of any co-operative group set his heart upon the achievement of the same definite end, in a spirit of perfect harmony, and the way has been paved for the development of a Master Mind, providing all members of the group willingly subordinate their own personal interests for the attainment of the objective for which the group is aiming.

The United States of America has become one of the most powerful nations on earth, largely because of the highly organized co-operative effort between the states. It will be helpful to remember that these United States were born as the result of one of the most powerful Master Minds ever created. The members of this Master Mind were the signers of the Declaration of Independence.

The men who signed that document either consciously or unconsciously put into operation the power known as the "Master Mind," and that power was sufficient to enable them to defeat all the soldiers who were sent into the field against them. The men who fought to make the Declaration of Independence endure did not fight for money, alone; they fought for a principle—the principle of freedom, which is the highest known motivating force.

I do not know for sure, but I strongly suspect that the person who performs service that is greater in quantity and better in quality than that for which he is paid, is eventually paid for more than he performs.

A great leader, whether in business, finance, industry or statesmanship, is one who understands how to create a motivating objective which will be accepted with enthusiasm by every member of his group of followers.

In politics a "live issue" is everything!

By "live issue" is meant some popular objective toward the attainment of which the majority of the voters can be rallied. These "issues" generally are broadcast in the form of snappy slogans, such as "Keep Cool with Coolidge," which suggested to the minds of the voters that to keep Coolidge was the equivalent of keeping prosperity. It worked!

During Lincoln's election campaign the cry was, "Stand back of Lincoln and preserve the Union." It worked.

Woodrow Wilson's campaign managers, during his second campaign, coined the slogan, "He kept us out of war," and it worked.

The degree of power created by the co-operative effort of any group of people is measured, always, by the nature of the motive which the group is laboring to attain. This may be profitably borne in mind by all who organize group effort for any purpose whatsoever. Find a motive around which men may be induced to rally in a highly emotionalized, enthusiastic spirit of perfect harmony and you have found the starting point for the creation of a Master Mind.

It is a well known fact that men will work harder for the attainment of an ideal than they will for mere money. In searching for a "motive" as the basis for developing co-operative group effort it will be profitable to bear this fact in mind.

At the time of the writing of this lesson there is much adverse agitation and general criticism directed against the railroads of the country. Who is back of this agitation this author does not know, but he does know that the very fact that such agitation exists could and should be made the motivating force around which the railroad officials might rally the hundreds of thousands of railroad employees who earn their living by railroading, thereby creating a power that would effectively eliminate this adverse criticism.

The railroads are the very back-bone of the country. Tie up all railroad service and the people of the larger cities would starve before food could reach them. In this fact may be found a motive around which a large majority of the public could be caused to rally in support of any plan for self-protection which the railroad officials might wish to carry out.

The power represented by all of the railroad employees and a majority of the public who patronize the railroads is sufficient to protect the railroads against all manner of adverse legislation and other attempts to depreciate their properties, but the power is only potential until it is organized and placed definitely back of a specific motive.

Man is a queer animal. Give him a sufficiently vitalized motive and the man of but average ability, under ordinary circumstances, will suddenly develop superpower.

What man can and will accomplish to please the woman of his choice (providing the woman knows how to stimulate him to action) has ever been a source of wonderment to students of the human mind.

There are three major motivating forces to which man responds in practically all of his efforts. These are:

1. The motive of self-preservation
2. The motive of sexual contact
3. The motive of financial and social power.

Stated more briefly, the main motives which impel men to action are money, sex and self-preservation. Leaders who are seeking a motivating force out of which to secure action from a following may find it under one or more of these three classifications.

As you have observed, this lesson is very closely related to the Introductory Lesson and Lesson Two which cover the Law of the Master Mind. It is possible for groups to function co-operatively, without thereby creating a Master Mind, as, for example, where people co-operate merely out of necessity, without the spirit of harmony as the basis of their efforts, This sort of co-operation may produce considerable power, but nothing to compare with that which is possible when every person in an alliance subordinates his or her own individual interests and co-ordinates his or her efforts with those of all other members of the alliance, in perfect harmony.

> *Your position is nothing more than your opportunity to show what sort of ability you have. You will get out of it exactly what you put into it — no more and no less. A "big" position is but the sum total of numerous "little" positions well filled.*

The extent to which people may be induced to cooperate, in harmony, depends upon the motivating force which impels them to action. Perfect harmony such as is essential for creating a Master Mind can be obtained only when the motivating force of a group is sufficient to cause each member of the group completely to forget his or her own personal interests and work for the good of the group, or for the sake of attaining some idealistic, charitable or philanthropic objective.

The three major motivating forces of mankind have been here stated for the guidance of the Leader who wishes to create plans for securing co-operation from followers who will throw themselves into the carrying out of his plans in a spirit of unselfishness and perfect harmony.

Men will not rally to the support of a leader in such a spirit of harmony unless the motive that impels them to do so is one that will induce them to lay aside all thoughts of themselves.

We do well that which we love to do, and fortunate is the Leader who has the good judgment to bear this fact in mind and so lay his plans that all his followers are assigned parts that harmonize with this law.

The leader who gets all thee is to be had from his followers does so because he has set up in the mind of each a sufficiently strong motive to get each to sub-ordinate his own interests and work in a perfect spirit of harmony with all other members of the group.

Regardless of who you are, or what your *definite chief aim* may be, if you plan to attain the object of your *chief aim* through the co-operative efforts of others you must set up in the minds of those whose co-operation you seek a motive strong enough to insure their full, undivided, unselfish co-operation, for you will then be placing back of your plans the power of the Law of the Master Mind.

You are now ready to take up Lesson Fourteen, which will teach you how to make working capital out of all mistakes, errors and failures which you have experienced, and also how to profit by the mistakes and failures of others.

The president of one of the great railway systems of the United States said, after reading the next lesson, that "this lesson carries a suggestion which, if heeded and understood, will enable any person to become a master in his chosen life-work."

For reasons which will be plain after you have read the next lesson, it is the author's favorite lesson of this course.

YOUR STANDING ARMY

AN AFTER-THE-LESSON VISIT WITH THE AUTHOR

These fifteen soldiers are labeled: Definite Chief Aim, Self-Confidence, Habit of Saving, Imagination, Initiative and Leadership, Enthusiasm, Self-Control, Doing More Than Paid For, Pleasing Personality, Accurate Thought, Concentration, Co-operation, Failure, Tolerance, Golden Rule

Power comes from organized effort. You see in the above picture the forces which enter into all organized effort. Master these fifteen forces and you may have whatever you want in life. Others will be helpless to defeat your plans. Make these fifteen forces your own and you will be an accurate thinker.

IN THE PICTURE at the top of this page you see the most powerful army on earth! Observe the emphasis on the word POWERFUL.

This army is standing at attention, ready to do the bidding of any person who will command it. It is YOUR army if you will take charge of it.

This army will give you POWER sufficient to mow down all opposition with which you meet. Study the picture carefully, then take inventory of yourself and find out how many of these soldiers you need.

✦

If you are a normal person you long for material success.

Success and POWER are always found together. You cannot be sure of success unless you have power. You cannot have power unless you develop it through fifteen essential qualities.

Each of these fifteen qualities may be likened to the commanding officer of a regiment of soldiers. Develop these qualities in your own mind and you will have POWER.

The most important of the fifteen commanding officers in this army is DEFINITE PURPOSE.

Without the aid of a definite purpose the remainder of the army would be useless to you. Find out, as early in life as possible, what your major purpose in life shall be. Until you do this you are nothing but a drifter, subject to control by every stray wind of circumstance that blows in your direction.

Millions of people go through life without knowing what it is they want.

All have a purpose, but only two out of every hundred have a DEFINITE purpose. Before you decide whether your purpose is DEFINITE or not, look up the meaning of the word in the dictionary.

NOTHING IS IMPOSSIBLE TO THE PERSON WHO KNOWS WHAT IT IS HE WANTS AND MAKES UP HIS MIND TO ACQUIRE IT!

Columbus had a DEFINITE PURPOSE and it became a reality. Lincoln's major DEFINITE PURPOSE was to free the black slaves of the South and he turned that purpose into reality. Roosevelt's major purpose, during his first term of office, was to build the Panama Canal. He lived to see that purpose realized. Henry Ford's DEFINITE PURPOSE was to build the best popular priced automobile on earth.

That purpose, backed persistently, has made him the most powerful man on earth. Burbank's DEFINITE PURPOSE was to improve plant life. Already that purpose has made possible the raising of enough food on ten square miles of land to feed the entire world.

Twenty years ago Edwin C. Barnes formed a DEFINITE PURPOSE in his mind. That purpose was to become the business partner of Thomas A. Edison. At the time his purpose was chosen Mr. Barnes had no qualification entitling him to a partnership with the world's greatest inventor. Despite this handicap he became the partner of the great Edison. Five years ago he retired from active business, with more money than he needs or can use, wealth that he accumulated in partnership with Edison.

NOTHING IS IMPOSSIBLE TO THE MAN WITH A DEFINITE PURPOSE!

Opportunity, capital, co-operation from other men and all other essentials for success gravitate to the man who knows what he wants!

Vitalize your mind with a DEFINITE PURPOSE and immediately your mind becomes a magnet which attracts everything that harmonizes with that purpose,

James J. Hill, the great railroad builder, was a poorly paid telegraph operator. Moreover, he had reached the age of forty and was still ticking away at the telegraph key without any outward appearances of success.

Then something of importance happened! Of importance to Hill and to the people of the United States. He formed the DEFINITE PURPOSE of building a railroad across the great waste desert of the West. Without reputation, without capital, without encouragement from others James J. Hill got the capital and built the greatest of all the railroad systems of the United States.

Woolworth was a poorly paid clerk in a general store. In his mind's eye he saw a chain of novelty stores specializing on five and ten cent sales. That chain of stores became his DEFINITE PURPOSE. He made that purpose come true, and with it more millions than he could use.

Cyrus H. K. Curtis selected, as his DEFINITE PURPOSE, the publishing of the world's greatest magazine. Starting with nothing but the name "Saturday Evening Post," and opposed by friends and advisers who said "It couldn't be done," he transformed that purpose into reality.

Martin W. Littleton is the most highly paid lawyer in the world. It is said that he will accept no retainer under $50,000.00. When he was twelve years old he had never been inside of a school house. He went to hear a lawyer defend a murderer. That speech so impressed him that he grabbed hold of his father's hand and said, "Some day I am going to be the best lawyer in the United States and make speeches like that man."

"Fine chance for an ignorant mountain youth to become a great lawyer," someone might say, but remember that NOTHING IS IMPOSSIBLE TO THE MAN WHO KNOWS WHAT HE WANTS AND MAKES UP HIS MIND TO GET IT.

Study each of the fifteen soldiers shown in command of the army in the picture at the beginning of this essay.

Remember, as you look at the picture, that no one of these soldiers alone is powerful enough to insure success. Remove a single one of them and the entire army would be weakened.

The powerful man is the man who has developed, in his own mind, the entire fifteen qualities represented by the fifteen commanding officers shown in the picture. Before you can have power you must have a DEFINITE PURPOSE; you must have SELF-CONFIDENCE with which to back up that purpose; you must have INITIATIVE and LEADERSHIP with which to exercise your self-confidence; you must have IMAGINATION in creating your definite purpose and in building the plans with which to transform that purpose into reality and put your plans into action. You must mix ENTHUSIASM with your action or it will be insipid and without "kick." You must exercise SELF-CONTROL. You must form the habit of DOING MORE THAN PAID FOR. You must cultivate a PLEASING PERSONALITY. You must acquire the HABIT OF SAVING.

You must become an ACCURATE THINKER, remembering, as you develop this quality, that accurate thought is based upon FACTS and not upon hearsay evidence or mere information. You must form the habit of CONCENTRATION by giving your undivided attention to but one task at a time. You must acquire the habit of CO-OPERATION and practice it in all your plans. You must profit by FAILURE, your own and that of others. You must cultivate the habit of TOLERANCE. Last, but by no means the least important, you must make the GOLDEN RULE the foundation of all you do that affects other people.

Keep this picture where you can see it each day and, one by one, call these fifteen soldiers out of the line and study them. Make sure that the counterpart of each is developed in your own mind.

All efficient armies are well disciplined!

The army which you are building in your own mind must, also, be disciplined. It must obey your command at every step.

When you call out of the line the thirteenth soldier, "FAILURE," remember that nothing will go as far toward developing discipline as will failure and temporary defeat. While you are comparing yourself with this soldier determine whether or not you have been profiting by your own failures and temporary defeat.

FAILURE comes to all at one time or another. Make sure, when it comes your way, that you will learn something of value from its visit. Make sure, also, that it would not visit you if there was not room for it in your make-up.

To make progress in this world you must rely solely upon the forces within your own mind for your start. After this start has been made you may turn to others for aid, but the first step must be taken without outside aid.

After you have made this "start," it will surprise you to observe how many willing people you will encounter who will volunteer to assist you.

Success is made up of many facts and factors, chiefly of the fifteen qualities represented by these fifteen soldiers. To enjoy a well balanced and rounded out success one must appropriate as much or as little of each of these fifteen qualities as may be missing in one's own inherited ability.

When you came into this world you were endowed with certain inborn traits, the result of millions of years of evolutionary changes, through thousands of generations of ancestors.

Added to these inborn traits you acquired many other qualities, according to the nature of your environment and the teaching you received during your early childhood. You are the sum total of that which was born in you and that which you have picked up from your experiences, what you have thought and what you have been taught, since birth.

Through the law of chance one in a million people will receive, through inborn heredity and from knowledge acquired after birth, all of the fifteen qualities named in the picture above.

All who are not fortunate enough to have thus acquired the essentials for SUCCESS must develop them within themselves.

The first step in this "development" process is to realize what qualities are missing in your naturally acquired equipment. The second step is the strongly planted DESIRE to develop yourself where you are now deficient.

Prayer sometimes works, while at other times it does not work.

It always works when backed with unqualified FAITH. This is a truth which no one will deny, yet, it is a truth which no one can explain. All we know is that prayer works when we BELIEVE it will work. Prayer without FAITH is nothing but an empty collection of words.

A DEFINITE PURPOSE may be transformed into reality only when one BELIEVES it can be done. Perhaps the selfsame law that turns the prayer based upon FAITH into reality transforms, also, a DEFINITE PURPOSE that is founded upon belief into reality.

It can do no harm if you make your DEFINITE PURPOSE in life the object of your daily prayer. And, as you pray remember that prayer based upon FAITH always works.

Develop in your own mind all of the fifteen qualities, from a DEFINITE PURPOSE to the GOLDEN RULE, and you will find the application of FAITH is not difficult.

Take inventory of yourself. Find out how many of the fifteen qualities you now possess. Add to this inventory the missing qualities until you have, in your mind, the entire fifteen. You will then be ready to measure your success in whatever terms you DESIRE.

The qualities represented by the fifteen soldiers shown in this picture are the brick and the mortar and the building material with which you must build your Temple of Success. Master these fifteen qualities and you may play a perfect symphony of success in any undertaking, just as one who has mastered the fundamentals of music may play any piece at sight.

Make these fifteen qualities your own and you will be an EDUCATED person, because you will have the power to get whatever you want in life without violating the rights of others.

All worlds are man's, to conquer and to rule
　　This is the glory of his life.
But this its iron law: first must he school
　　Himself. Here 'gins and ends all strife.

FAILURE

Yesterday is but a dream,

Tomorrow is only a vision.

But today well lived makes

Every yesterday a dream of happiness,

And every tomorrow a vision of hope.

Look well, therefore, to this day.

—From the Sanskrit

You Can Do It If You Believe You Can!

UNDER ORDINARY CIRCUMSTANCES the term "failure" is a negative term. In this lesson, the word will be given a new meaning, because the word has been a very much misused one; and, for that reason, it has brought unnecessary grief and hardship to millions of people.

In the outset, let us distinguish between "failure" and "temporary defeat." Let us see if that which is so often looked upon as "failure" is not, in reality, but "temporary defeat." Moreover, let us see if this temporary defeat is not usually a blessing in disguise, for the reason that it brings us up with a jerk and redirects our energies along different and more desirable lines.

In Lesson Nine of this course, we learned that strength grows out of resistance; and we shall learn, in this lesson, that sound character is usually the handiwork of reverses, and set-backs, and temporary defeat, which the uninformed part of the world calls "failure."

Neither temporary defeat nor adversity amounts to failure in the mind of the person who looks upon it as a teacher that will teach some needed lesson. As a matter of fact, there is a great and lasting lesson in every reverse, and in every defeat; and, usually, it is a lesson that could be learned in no other way than through defeat.

Defeat often talks to us in a "dumb language" that we do not understand. If this were not true, we would not make the same mistakes over and over again without profiting by the lessons that they might teach us. If it were not true, we would observe more closely the mistakes which other people make and profit by them.

The main object of this lesson is to help the student understand and profit by this "dumb language" in which defeat talks to us.

Perhaps I can best help you to interpret the meaning of defeat by taking you back over some of my own experiences covering a period of approximately thirty years. Within this period, I have come to the turning-point, which the uninformed call "failure," seven different times. At each of these seven turning-points I thought I had made a dismal failure; but now I know that what looked to be a failure was nothing more than a kindly, unseen hand, that halted me in my chosen course and with great wisdom forced me to redirect my efforts along more advantageous pathways.

I arrived at this decision, however, only after I had taken a retrospective view of my experiences and had analyzed them in the light of many years of sober and meditative thought.

First Turning-Point

After finishing a course in a business college, I secured a position as stenographer and bookkeeper which I held for the ensuing five years. As a result of having practiced the habit of performing more work and better work than that for which I was paid, as described in Lesson Nine of this course, I advanced rapidly until I was assuming responsibilities and receiving a salary far out of proportion to my age. I saved my money; and my bank account amounted to several thousand dollars. My reputation spread rapidly and I found competitive bidders for my services.

To meet these offers from competitors my employer advanced me to the position of General Manager of the mines where I was employed. I was quickly getting on top of the world, and *I knew it!*

Ah! but that was the sad part of my fate—*I knew it!*

Then the kindly hand of Fate reached out and gave me a gentle nudge. My employer lost his fortune and I lost my position. This was my first real defeat; and, even though it came about as a result of causes beyond my control, I should have learned a lesson from it; which, of course, I did, but not until many years later.

Second Turning-Point

My next position was that of Sales Manager for a large lumber manufacturing concern in the South. I knew nothing about lumber, and but little about sales management; but I had learned that it was beneficial to render more service than that for which I was paid; and I had also learned that it paid to take the initiative and find out what ought to be done without someone telling me to do it. A good sized bank account, plus a record of steady advancement in my previous position, gave me all the self-confidence I needed, with some to spare, perhaps.

My advancement was rapid, my salary having been increased twice during the first year. I did so well in the management of sales that my employer took me into partnership with him. We began to make money and I began to see myself *on top of the world again!*

To stand "on top of the world" gives one a wonderful sensation; but it is a very dangerous place to stand, unless one stands very firmly, because the fall is so long and hard if one should stumble.

I was succeeding by leaps and bounds!

Up to that time it had never occurred to me that *success* could be measured in terms other than money and authority. Perhaps this was due to the fact that I had more money than I needed and more authority than I could manage safely at that age.

Not only was I "succeeding," from my viewpoint of success, but I knew I was engaged in the one and only business suited to my temperament. Nothing could have induced me to change into another line of endeavor. That is—nothing except that which happened, which *forced* me to change.

The unseen hand of Fate allowed me to strut around under the influence of my own vanity until I had commenced to feel my importance. In the light of my more sober years, I now wonder if the Unseen Hand does not purposely permit us foolish human beings to parade ourselves before our own mirrors of vanity until we come to see how vulgarly we are acting and become ashamed of ourselves. At any rate, I seemed to have a clear track ahead of me; there was plenty of coal in the bunker; there was water in the tank; my hand was on the throttle—I opened it wide and sped along at a rapid pace.

Alas! Fate awaited me just around the corner, with a stuffed club that was not stuffed with cotton. Of course I did not see the impending crash until it came. Mine was a sad story, but not unlike that which many another might tell if he would be frank with himself.

Like a stroke of lightning out of a clear sky, the 1907 panic swept down upon me; and, overnight, it rendered me an enduring service by destroying my business and relieving me of every dollar that I possessed.

This was my first serious *defeat!* I mistook it, then, for failure; but it was not, and before I complete this lesson I will tell you why it was not.

THIRD TURNING-POINT

It required the 1907 panic, and the defeat that it brought me, to divert and redirect my efforts from the lumber business to the study of law. Nothing on earth, except defeat, could have brought about this result; thus, the third turning-point of my life was ushered in on the wings of that which most people would call "failure," which reminds me to state again that every defeat teaches a needed lesson to those who are ready and willing to be taught.

When I entered law school, it was with the firm belief that I would emerge doubly prepared to catch up with the end of the rainbow and claim my pot of gold; for I still had no other conception of success except that of *money* and power.

I attended law school at night and worked as an automobile salesman during the day. My sales experience in the lumber business was turned to good advantage. I prospered rapidly, doing so well (still featuring the habit of performing more service and better service than that for which I was paid) that the opportunity came to enter the automobile manufacturing business. I saw the need for trained automobile mechanics, therefore I opened an educational department in the manufacturing plant and began to train ordinary machinists in automobile assembling and repair work. The school prospered, paying me over a thousand dollars a month in net profits.

One of the greatest leaders who ever lived stated the secret of his leadership in six words, as follows: "Kindness is more powerful than compulsion."

Again I was beginning to near the end of the rainbow. Again I knew I had at last found my niche in the world's work; that nothing could swerve me from my course or divert my attention from the automobile business.

My banker knew that I was prospering, therefore he loaned me money with which to expand. A peculiar trait of bankers—a trait which may be more or less developed in the remainder of us also—is that they will loan us money without any hesitation when we are *prosperous!*

My banker loaned me money until I was hopelessly in his debt, then he took over my business as calmly as if it had belonged to him, which it did!

From the station of a man of affairs who enjoyed an income of more than a thousand dollars a month, I was suddenly reduced to poverty.

Now, twenty years later, I thank the hand of Fate for this forced change; but at that time I looked upon the change as nothing but *failure*.

The rainbow's end had disappeared, and with it the proverbial pot of gold which is supposed to be found at its end. It was many years afterwards that I learned the truth that this temporary *defeat* was probably the greatest single blessing that ever came my way, because it forced me out of a business that in no way helped me to develop knowledge of self or of others, and directed my efforts into a channel which brought me a rich experience of which I was in need.

For the first time in life I began to ask myself if it were not possible for one to find something of value other than money and power at the rainbow's end. This temporary questioning attitude did not amount to open rebellion, mind you, nor did I follow it far enough to get the answer. It merely came as a fleeting thought, as do so many other thoughts to which we pay no attention, and passed out of my mind. Had I known as much then as I now know about the Law of Compensation, and had I been able to interpret experiences as I can now interpret them, I would have recognized that event as a gentle nudge from the hand of Fate.

After putting up the hardest fight of my life, up to that time, I accepted my temporary defeat as *failure* and thus was ushered in my next and fourth turning-point, which gave me an opportunity to put into use the knowledge of law that I had acquired.

FOURTH TURNING-POINT

Because I was my wife's husband and her people had influence I secured the appointment as assistant to the chief counsel for one of the largest coal companies in the world. My salary was greatly out of proportion to those usually paid to beginners, and still further out of proportion to what I was worth; but pull was pull, and I was there just the same. It happened that what I lacked in legal skill I more than made up through the application of the principle of performing more service than that for which I was paid, and by taking the initiative and doing that which should have been done without being told to do it.

I was holding my position without difficulty. I practically had a soft berth for life had I cared to keep it.

Without consultation with my friends, and without warning, I resigned!

This was the first turning-point that was of my own selection. It was not forced upon me. I saw the old man Fate coming and beat him to the door. When pressed for a reason for resigning, I gave what seemed to me to be a very sound one, but I had trouble convincing the family circle that I had acted wisely.

I quit that position because the work was too easy and I was performing it with too little effort. I saw myself drifting into the habit of inertia. I felt myself becoming accustomed to taking life easily and I knew that the next step would be retrogression. I had so many friends at court that there was no particular impelling urge that made it necessary for me to keep moving. I was among friends and relatives, and I had a position that I could keep as long as I wished it, without exerting myself. I received an income that provided me with all the necessities and some of the luxuries, including a motor car and enough gasoline to keep it running.

What more did I need?

"Nothing," I was beginning to say to myself.

This was the attitude toward which I felt myself slipping. It was an attitude which, for some reason that is still unknown to me, startled me so sharply that I made what many believed to be an irrational move by resigning. However ignorant I might have been in other matters at the time, I have felt thankful ever since for having had sense enough to realize that strength and growth come only through continuous effort and *struggle,* that disuse brings atrophy and decay.

This move proved to be the next most important turning-point of my life, although it was followed by ten years of effort which brought almost every conceivable grief that the human heart can experience. I quit my job in the legal field, where I was getting along well, living among friends and relatives, where I had what they believed to be an unusually bright and promising future ahead of me. I am frank to admit that it has been an ever-increasing source of wonderment to me as to why and how I gathered the courage to make the move that I did. As far as I am able to interpret the event, I arrived at my decision to resign more because of a "hunch," or a sort of "prompting" which I then did not understand, than by logical reasoning.

I selected Chicago as my new field of endeavor. I did this because I believed Chicago to be a place where one might find out if one had those sterner qualities which are so essential for survival in a world of keen competition. I made up my mind that if I could gain recognition, in any honorable sort of work, in Chicago, it would prove that I had the sort of material in my make-up that might be developed into real ability. That was a queer process of reasoning; at least it was an unusual process for me to indulge in at that time, which reminds me to state that we human beings often take unto ourselves credit for intelligence to which we are not entitled. I fear we too often assume credit for wisdom and for results that accrue from causes over which we have absolutely no control.

While I do not mean to convey the impression that I believe all of our acts to be controlled by causes beyond our power to direct, yet I strongly urge you to study and correctly interpret those causes which mark the most vital turning-points of your life; the points at which your efforts are diverted — from the old into new channels — in spite of all that you can do. *At least refrain from accepting any defeat as failure until you shall have had time to analyze the final result.*

My first position in Chicago was that of advertising manager of a large correspondence school. I knew but little about advertising, but my previous experience as a salesman, plus the advantage gained by rendering more service than that for which I was paid, enabled me to make an unusual showing.

The first year I earned $5,200.00.

I was "coming back" by leaps and bounds. Gradually the rainbow's end began to circle around me, and I saw, once more, the shining pot of gold almost within my reach. History is full of evidence that a feast usually precedes a famine. I was enjoying a feast but did not anticipate the famine that was to follow. I was getting along so well that I thoroughly approved of myself.

Self-approval is a dangerous state of mind.

This is a great truth which many people do not learn until the softening hand of Time has rested upon their shoulders for the better part of a life-time. Some never do learn it, and those who do are those who finally begin to understand the "dumb language" of defeat.

I am convinced that one has but few, if any, more dangerous enemies to combat than that of self-approval. Personally I fear it more than defeat.

Remember this, when things go against you, that of all the expressions you carry in your face the light of joy shines farthest out to sea.

This brings me to my fifth turning-point, which was also of my own choice.

Fifth Turning-Point

I had made such a good record as advertising manager of the correspondence school that the president of the school induced me to resign my position and go into the candy manufacturing business with him. We organized the Betsy Ross Candy Company and I became its first president, thus beginning the next most important turning-point of my life.

The business grew rapidly until we had a chain of stores in eighteen different cities. Again I saw my rainbow's end almost within my reach. I knew that I had at last found the business in which I wished to remain for life. The candy business was profitable and, because I looked upon money as being the only evidence of success, I naturally believed I was about to corner success.

Everything went smoothly until my business associate and a third man, whom we had taken into the business, took a notion to gain control of my interest in the business without paying for it.

Their plan was successful, in a way, but I balked more stiffly than they had anticipated I would; therefore, for the purpose of "gentle persuasion," they had me arrested on a false charge and then offered to withdraw the charge on condition that I turn over to them my interest in the business.

I had commenced to learn, for the first time, that there was much cruelty, and injustice, and dishonesty in the hearts of men.

When the time for a preliminary hearing came, the complaining witnesses were nowhere to be found. But I had them brought and forced them to go on the witness stand and tell their stories, which resulted in my vindication, and a damage suit against the perpetrators of the injustice.

This incident brought about an irreparable breach between my business associates and myself, which finally cost me my interest in the business, but that was but slight when compared to that which it cost my associates; for they are still paying, and no doubt will continue to pay as long as they live.

My damage suit was brought under what is known as a "tort" action, through which damages were claimed for malicious damage to character. In Illinois, where the action was brought, judgment under a tort action gives the one in favor of whom the judgment is rendered the right to have the person against whom it is obtained placed in jail until the amount of the judgment has been paid.

In due time I got a heavy judgment against my former business associates. *I could then have had both of them placed behind the bars.*

For the first time in my life I was brought face to face with the opportunity to strike back at my enemies in a manner that would hurt. I had in my possession a weapon with "teeth" in it—a weapon placed there by the enemies, themselves.

The feeling that swept over me was a queer one!

Would I have my enemies jailed, or would I take advantage of this opportunity to extend them mercy, thereby proving myself to be made of a different type of material.

Then and there was laid, in my heart, the foundation upon which the Sixteenth Lesson of this course is built, for I made up my mind to permit my enemies to go free—as free as they could be made by my having extended them mercy and forgiveness.

But long before my decision had been reached the hand of Fate had commenced to deal roughly with these misguided fellow men who had tried, in vain, to destroy me. Time, the master worker, to which we must all submit sooner or later, had already been at work on my former business associates, and it had dealt with them less mercifully than I had done. One of them was later sentenced to a long term in the penitentiary, for another crime that he had committed against some other person, and the other one had, meanwhile, been reduced to pauperism.

We can circumvent the laws which men place upon statute books, but the Law of Compensation never!

The judgment which I obtained against these men stands on the records of the Superior Court, of Chicago, as silent evidence of vindication of my character; but it serves me in a more important way than that—it serves as a reminder that I could forgive enemies who had tried to destroy me, and for this reason, instead of destroying my character, I suspect that the incident served to strengthen it.

Being arrested seemed, at the time, a terrible disgrace, even though the charge was false. I did not relish the experience, and I would not wish to go through a similar experience again, but I am bound to admit that it was worth all the grief it cost me, because it gave me the opportunity to find out that revenge was not a part of my make-up.

Here I would direct your attention to a close analysis of the events described in this lesson, for if you observe carefully you can see how this entire course of study has been evolved out of these experiences. Each temporary defeat left its mark upon my heart and provided some part of the material of which this course has been built.

We would cease to fear or to run away from trying experiences if we observed, from the biographies of men of destiny, that nearly every one of them was sorely tried and run through the mill of merciless experience before he "arrived." This leads me to wonder if the hand of Fate does not test "the metal of which we are made" in various and sundry ways before placing great responsibilities upon our shoulders.

Before approaching the next turning-point of my life, may I not call your attention to the significant fact that each turning-point carried me nearer and nearer my rainbow's end, and brought me some useful knowledge which became, later, a permanent part of my philosophy of life.

SIXTH TURNING-POINT

We come, now, to the turning-point which probably brought me nearer the rainbow's end than any of the others had, because it placed me in a position where I found it necessary to bring into use all the knowledge I had acquired up to that time, concerning practically every subject with which I was acquainted, and gave me opportunity for self-expression and development such as rarely comes to a man so early in life. This turning-point came shortly after my dreams of success in the candy business had been shattered, when I turned my efforts to teaching Advertising and Salesmanship as a department of one of the colleges of the Middle West.

Some wise philosopher has said that we never learn very much about a given subject until we commence teaching it to others. My first experience as a teacher proved this to be true. My school prospered from the very beginning. I had a resident class and also a correspondence school through which I was teaching students in nearly every English-speaking country. Despite the ravages of war, the school was growing rapidly and I again saw the end of the rainbow within sight.

Then came the second military draft which practically destroyed my school, as it caught most of those who were enrolled as students. At one stroke I charged off more than $75,000.00 in tuition fees and at the same time contributed my own service to my country.

Once more I was penniless!

Unfortunate is the person who has never had the thrill of being penniless at one time or another; for, as Edward Bok has truthfully stated, poverty is the richest experience that can come to a man; an experience which, however, he advises one to get away from as quickly as possible.

Again I was forced to redirect my efforts, but, before I proceed to describe the next and last important turning-point, I wish to call your attention to the fact that no single event described up to this point is, within itself, of any practical significance. The six turning-points that I have briefly described meant nothing to me, taken singly, and they will mean nothing to you if analyzed singly. But take these events collectively and they form a very significant foundation for the next turning-point, and constitute reliable evidence that we human beings are constantly undergoing evolutionary changes as a result of the experiences of life with which we meet, even though no single experience may seem to convey a definite, usable lesson.

It is far better to be associated with a few who are right than with the mob which is wrong, because right is always the winner in the end.

I feel impelled to dwell at length on the point which I am here trying to make clear, because I have now reached the point in my career at which men go down in permanent defeat or rise, with renewed energies, to heights of attainment of stupendous proportions, according to the manner in which they interpret their past experiences and use those experiences as the basis of working plans. If my story stopped here it would be of no value to you, but there is another and a more significant chapter yet to be written, covering the seventh and most important of all the turning-points of my life.

It must have been obvious to you, all through my description of the six turning-points already outlined, that I had not really found my place in the world. It must have been obvious to you that most, if not all, of my temporary defeats were due mainly to the fact that I had not yet discovered the work into which I could throw my heart and soul. Finding the work for which one is best fitted and which one likes best is very much like finding the one person whom one loves best; there is no rule by which to make the search, but when the right niche is contacted one immediately recognizes it. I too was able to recognize immediately the work I was best fitted for.

Seventh Turning-Point

Before I finish I will describe the collective lessons that I learned from each of the seven turning-points of my life, but first let me describe the seventh and last of these turning-points. To do so, I must go back to that eventful day—*November 11, 1918!*

That was Armistice Day, the end of World War I. The war had left me without a penny, as I have stated, but I was happy to know that the slaughter had ceased and reason was about to reclaim civilization once more.

As I stood in front of my office window and looked out at the howling mob that was celebrating the end of the war, my mind went back into my yesterdays, especially to that eventful day when that kind old gentleman laid his hand on my shoulder and told me that if I would acquire an education I could make my mark in the world. I had been acquiring that education without knowing it. Over a period of more than twenty years I had been going to school in the University of Hard Knocks, as you must have observed from my description of the various turning-points of my life. As I stood in front of that window my entire past, with its bitter and its sweet, its ups and its downs, passed before me in review.

The time had come for another turning-point!

I sat down to my typewriter and, to my astonishment, my hands began to play a regular tune upon the key-board. I had never written so rapidly or so easily before. I did not plan or think about that which I was writing—*I just wrote that which came into my mind!*

Unconsciously, I was laying the foundation for the most important turning-point of my life; for, when I had finished, I had prepared a document through which I financed a national magazine that gave me contact with people throughout the English-speaking world. So greatly did that document influence my own career, and the lives of tens of thousands of other people, that I believe it will be of interest to the students of this course; therefore, I am reproducing it, just as it appeared in *Hill's Golden Rule* magazine, where it was first published, as follows:

A PERSONAL VISIT WITH YOUR EDITOR

I am writing on Monday, November eleventh, 1918. Today will go down in history as the greatest holiday.

On the street, just outside of my office window, the surging crowds of people are celebrating the downfall of an influence that has menaced civilization for the past four years.

The war is over!

Soon our boys will be coming back home from the battle-fields of France.

The lord and master of Brute Force is nothing but a shadowy ghost of the past!

Two thousand years ago the Son of man was an outcast, with no place of abode. Now the situation has been reversed and the devil has no place to lay his head.

Let each of us take unto himself the great lesson that this world war has taught; namely, only that which is based upon justice and mercy toward all—the weak and the strong, the rich and the poor, alike—can survive. All else must pass on.

Out of this war will come a new idealism—an idealism that will be based upon the Golden Rule philosophy; an idealism that will guide us, not to see how much we can "do our fellow man for"; but how much we can do for him that will ameliorate his hardships and make him happier as he tarries by the wayside of life.

Emerson embodied this idealism in his great essay, the "Law of Compensation." Another great Philosopher embodied it in these words, "Whatsoever a man soweth, that shall he also reap."

The time for practicing the Golden Rule philosophy is upon us. In business as well as in social relationships he who neglects or refuses to use this philosophy as the basis of his dealings will but hasten the time of his failure.

And, while I am intoxicated with the glorious news of the war's ending, is it not fitting that I should attempt to do something to help preserve for the generations yet to come, one of the great lessons to be learned from William Hohenzollern's effort to rule the earth by *force?*

I can best do this by going back twenty-two years for my beginning. Come with me, won't you?

It was a bleak November morning, probably not far from the eleventh of the month, that I got my first job as a laborer in the coal mine regions of Virginia, at wages of a dollar a day.

A dollar a day was a big sum in those days; especially to a boy of my age. Of this, I paid fifty cents a day for my board and room.

Shortly after I began work, the miners became dissatisfied and commenced talking about striking. I listened eagerly to all that was said. I was especially interested in the organizer who had organized the union. He was one of the smoothest speakers I had ever heard, and his words fascinated me. He said one thing, in particular, that I have never forgotten; and, if I knew where to find him, I would look him up today and thank him warmly for saying it. The philosophy which I gathered from his words has had a most profound and enduring influence upon me.

Perhaps you will say that most labor agitators are not very sound philosophers; and I would agree with you if you said so. Maybe this one was not a sound philosopher, but surely the philosophy he expounded on this occasion was sound.

Standing on a dry goods box, in the corner of an old shop where he was holding a meeting, he said:

"Men, we are talking about striking. Before you vote I wish to call your attention to something that will benefit you if you will heed what I say.

> *No one is living aright unless he so lives that whoever meets him goes away more confident and joyous for the contact.*
>
> *–Lilian Whiting*

"You want more money for your work; and I wish to see you get it, because I believe you deserve it.

"May I not tell you how to get more money and still retain the good-will of the owner of this mine?

"We can call a strike and probably force them to pay more money, but we cannot force them to do this and like it. Before we call a strike, let us be fair with the owner of the mine and with ourselves; let us go to the owner and ask him if he will divide the profits of his mine with us fairly.

"If he says 'yes,' as he probably will, then let us ask him how much he made last month and, if he will divide among us a fair proportion of any additional profits he may make if we all jump in and help him earn more next month.

"He, being human, like each of us, will no doubt say—'Why, certainly boys; go to it and I'll divide with you.' It is but natural that he would say that, boys.

"After he agrees to the plan, as I believe he will if we make him see that we are in earnest, I want every one of you to come to work with a smile on your face for the next thirty days. I want to hear you whistling a tune as you go into the mines. I want you to go at your work with the feeling that you are one of the partners in this business.

"Without hurting yourself you can do almost twice as much work as you are doing; and if you do more work, you are sure to help the owner of this mine make more money. And if he makes more money he will be glad to divide a part of it with you. He will do this for sound business reasons if not out of a spirit of fair play.

"He will retaliate as surely as there is a God above us. If he doesn't, I'll be personally responsible to you, and if you say so I'll help blow this mine into smithereens!

"That's how much I think of the plan, boys! Are you with me?"

They were, to the man!

Those words sank into my heart as though they had been burned there with a red-hot iron.

The following month every man in the mines received a bonus of twenty per cent of his month's earnings. Every month thereafter each man received a bright red envelope with his part of the extra earnings in it. On the outside of the envelope were these printed words:

Your part of the profits from the work which you did that you were not paid to do.

I have gone through some pretty tough experiences since those days of twenty-odd years ago, but I have always come out on top—a little wiser, a little happier, and a little better prepared to be of service to my fellow men, owing to my having applied the principle of performing more work than I was actually paid to perform.

It may be of interest to you to know that the last position I held in the coal business was that of Assistant to the Chief Counsel for one of the largest companies in the world. It is a considerable jump from the position of common laborer in the coal mines to that of Assistant to the Chief Counsel of one of the largest companies—a jump that I never could have made without the aid of this principle of performing more work than I was paid to perform.

I wish I had the space in which to tell you of the scores of times that this idea of performing more work than I was paid to perform has helped me over rough spots.

Many have been the times that I have placed an employer so deeply in my debt, through the aid of this principle, that I got whatever I asked for, without hesitation or quibbling; without complaint or hard feelings; and, what is more important, without the feeling that I was taking unfair advantage of my employer.

I believe most earnestly that anything a man acquires from his fellow man without the full consent of the one from whom it is acquired, will eventually burn a hole in his pocket, or blister the palms of his hands, to say nothing of gnawing at his conscience until his heart aches with regret.

As I said in the beginning, I am writing on the morning of the Eleventh of November, while the crowds are celebrating the great victory of *right* over *wrong!*

Therefore, it is but natural that I should turn to the silence of my heart for some thought to pass on to the world today—some thought that will help keep alive in the minds of Americans the spirit of idealism for which they have fought and in which they entered the world war.

I find nothing more appropriate than the philosophy which I have related, because I earnestly believe it was the arrogant disregard of this philosophy that brought Germany—the Kaiser and his people—to grief. To get this philosophy into the hearts of those who need it I shall publish a magazine to be called *Hill's Golden Rule.*

It takes money to publish national magazines, and I haven't very much of it at this writing; but before another month shall have passed, through the aid of the philosophy that I have tried to emphasize here, I shall find someone who will supply the necessary money and make it possible for me to pass on to the world the simple philosophy that lifted me out of the dirty coal mines and gave me a place where I can be of service to humanity. The philosophy which will raise you, my dear reader, whoever you may be and whatever you may be doing, into whatever position in life you may make up your mind to attain.

Every person has, or ought to have, the inherent desire to own something of monetary value. In at least a vague sort of way, every person who works for others (and this includes practically all of us) looks forward to the time when he will have some sort of a business or a profession of his own.

The best way to realize that ambition is to perform more work than one is paid to perform. You can get along with but little schooling; you can get along with but little capital; you can overcome almost any obstacle with which you are confronted, if you are honestly and earnestly willing to do the best work of which you are capable, regardless of the amount of money you receive for it....

[Note: It is the afternoon of November the twenty-first, just ten days since I wrote the foregoing editorial. I have just read it to George B. Williams, of Chicago, a man who came up from the bottom through the aid of the philosophy of which I have written, and he has made the publication of Hill's Golden Rule *magazine possible.]*

It was in this somewhat dramatic manner that a desire which had lain dormant in my mind for nearly twenty years became translated into reality. During all that time I had wanted to become the editor of a newspaper. Back more than thirty years ago, when I was a very small boy, I used to "kick" the press for my father when he was publishing a small weekly newspaper, and I grew to love the smell of printer's ink.

Perhaps this desire was subconsciously gaining momentum all those years of preparation, while I was going through the experiences outlined in the turning-points of my life, until it had finally to burst forth in terms of action; or it may be that there was another plan, over which I had no control, that urged me on and on, never giving me any rest in any other line of work, until I began the publication of my first magazine. That point can be passed for the moment. The important thing to which I would direct your attention is the fact that I found my proper niche in the world's work and I was very happy over it.

Strangely enough, I entered upon this work with never a thought of looking for either the end of the rainbow or the proverbial pot of gold which is supposed to be found at its end. For the first time in my life, I seemed to realize, beyond room for doubt, that there was something else to be sought in life that was worth more than gold;

therefore, I went at my editorial work with but one main thought in mind—and I pause while you ponder over this thought:

And that thought was to render the world the best service of which I was capable, whether my efforts brought me a penny in return or not!

The publication of *Hill's Golden Rule* magazine brought me in contact with the thinking class of people all over the country. It gave me my big chance to be heard. The message of optimism and good-will among men that it carried became so popular that I was invited to go on a country-wide speaking tour during the early part of 1920, during which I had the privilege of meeting and talking with some of the most progressive thinkers of this generation. Contact with these people went a very long way toward giving me the courage to keep on doing the good work that I had started. This tour was a liberal education, within itself, because it brought me in exceedingly close contact with people in practically all walks of life, and gave me a chance to see that the United States of America was a pretty large country.

Comes, now, a description of the climax of the seventh turning-point of my life.

During my speaking tour I was sitting in a restaurant in Dallas, Texas, watching the hardest downpour of rain that I have ever seen. The water was pouring down over the plate-glass window in two great streams, and playing backward and forward from one of these streams to the other were little streams, making what resembled a great ladder of water.

As I looked at this unusual scene, the thought "flashed into my mind" that I would have a splendid lecture if I organized all that I had learned from the seven turning-points of my life and all I had learned from studying the lives of successful men, and offered it under the title of the "Magic Ladder to Success."

On the back of an envelope I outlined the fifteen points out of which this lecture was built, and later I worked these points into a lecture that was literally built from the temporary defeats described in the seven turning-points of my life.

All that I lay claim to knowing that is of value is represented by these fifteen points; and the material out of which this knowledge was gathered is nothing more or less than the knowledge that was *forced* upon me through experiences which have undoubtedly been classed, by some, as *failures!*

The reading course, of which this lesson is a part, is-but the sum total of that which I gathered through these "failures." If this course proves to be of value to you, as I hope it will, you may give the credit to those "failures" described in this lesson.

Perhaps you will wish to know what material, monetary benefits I have gained from these turning-points, for you probably realize that we are living in an age in which life is an irksome struggle for existence and none too pleasant for those who are cursed with poverty.

All right! I'll be frank with you.

To begin with, the estimated income from the sale of this course is all that I need, and this, despite the fact that I have insisted that my publishers apply the Ford philosophy and sell the course at a popular price that is within the reach of all who want it.

To give pleasure to a single heart by a single kind act is better than a thousand head-bowings in prayer.

– Saadi

In addition to the income from the sale of the course (which, please bear in mind, is but the sale of knowledge I have gathered through "failure"), I am now engaged in writing a series of illustrated editorials that is to be syndicated and published in the newspapers of the country. These editorials are based upon these same fifteen points as outlined in this course.

The estimated net income from the sale of the editorials is more than enough to care for my needs.

In addition to this I am now engaged in collaboration with a group of scientists, psychologists and business men, in writing a postgraduate course which will soon be available to all students who have mastered this more elementary course, covering not only the fifteen laws here outlined, from a more advanced viewpoint, but including still other laws which have but recently been discovered.

I have mentioned these facts only because I know what a common thing it is for all of us to measure success in terms of dollars, and to refuse, as unsound, all philosophy that does not foot up a good bank balance.

Practically all the past years of my life I have been poor—exceedingly poor—as far as bank balances were concerned. This condition has been, very largely, a matter of choice with me, because I have been putting the best of my time into the toilsome job of throwing off some of my ignorance and gathering in some of the knowledge of life of which I felt myself in need.

From the experiences described in these seven turning-points of my life, I have gathered a few golden threads of knowledge that I could have gained in no other way than through *defeat!*

My own experiences have led me to believe that the "dumb language" of *defeat* is the plainest and most effective language in the world, once one begins to understand it. I am almost tempted to say that I believe it to be the universal language in which Nature cries out to us when we will listen to no other language.

I am glad that I have experienced much defeat!

It has had the effect of tempering me with the courage to undertake tasks that I would never have begun had I been surrounded by protecting influences.

Defeat is a destructive force only when it is accepted as failure! When accepted as teaching some needed lesson it is always a blessing.

I used to hate my enemies!

That was before I learned how well they were serving me by keeping me everlastingly on the alert lest some weak spot in my character provide an opening through which they might damage me.

In view of what I have learned of the value of enemies, if I had none I would feel it my duty to create a few. They would discover my defects and point them out to me, whereas my friends, if they saw my weaknesses at all, would say nothing about them.

Of all Joaquin Miller's poems none expressed a nobler thought than did this one:

For Those Who Fail

"All honor to him who shall win a prize,"
The world has cried for a thousand years;
But to him who tries, and who fails and dies,
I give great honor, and glory, and tears:

Give glory and honor and pitiful tears
To all who fail in their deeds sublime;
Their ghosts are many in the van of years,
They were born with Time, in advance of Time.

Oh, great is the hero who wins a name,
But greater many and many a time
Some pale-faced fellow who dies in shame,
And lets God finish the thought sublime.

And great is the man with a sword undrawn,
And good is the man who refrains from wine;
But the man who fails and yet still fights on,
Lo, he is the twin-born brother of mine.

(From *The Complete Poetical Works of Joaquin Miller,*
The Whitaker & Ray Company, 1902)

There can be no failure for the man who "still fights on." A man has never failed until he accepts temporary defeat as failure. There is a wide difference between temporary defeat and failure; a difference I have tried to emphasize throughout this lesson.

In her poem entitled "When Nature Wants a Man," Angela Morgan expressed a great truth in support of the theory set out in this lesson, that adversity and defeat are generally blessings in disguise.

When Nature Wants a Man

When Nature wants to drill a man,
And thrill a man,
And skill a man,
When Nature wants to mould a man
To play the noblest part;
When she yearns with all her heart
To create so great and bold a man
That all the world shall praise—
Watch her methods, watch her ways!
How she ruthlessly perfects
Whom she royally elects;
How she hammers him and hurts him
And with mighty blows converts him
Into trial shapes of clay which only Nature understands—
While his tortured heart is crying and he lifts beseeching
        hands!—
How she bends, but never breaks,
When his good she undertakes …
How she uses whom she chooses
And with every purpose fuses him,
By every art induces him
To try his splendour out—
Nature knows what she's about.

When Nature wants to take a man
And shake a man
And wake a man;
When Nature wants to make a man
To do the Future's will;
When she tries with all her skill
And she yearns with all her soul
To create him large and whole …

With what cunning she prepares him!
How she goads and never spares him,
How she whets him, and she frets him
And in poverty begets him …
How she often disappoints
Whom she sacredly anoints,
With what wisdom she will hide him,
Never minding what betide him
Though his genius sob with slighting and his pride
    may not forget!
Bids him struggle harder yet.
Makes him lonely
So that only
God's high messages shall reach him,
So that she may surely teach him
What the Hierarchy planned.
Though he may not understand,
Gives him passions to command—
How remorselessly she spurs him,
With terrific ardor stirs him
When she poignantly prefers him!

When Nature wants to name a man
And fame a man
And tame a man;
When Nature wants to shame a man
To do his heavenly best …
When she tries the highest test
That her reckoning may bring—
When she wants a god or king!—
How she reins him and restrains him
So his body scarce contains him
While she fires him
And inspires him!

Keeps him yearning, ever burning for a tantalising goal—
Lures and lacerates his soul.
Sets a challenge for his spirit,
Draws it higher when he's near it—
Makes a jungle, that he clear it;
Makes a desert that he fear it
And subdue it if he can—
So doth Nature make a man.
Then, to test his spirit's wrath
Hurls a mountain in his path—
Puts a bitter choice before him
And relentlessly stands o'er him.
"Climb, or perish!" so she says …
Watch her purpose, watch her ways!

Nature's plan is wondrous kind
Could we understand her mind …
Fools are they who call her blind.
When his feet are torn and bleeding
Yet his spirit mounts unheeding,
All his higher powers speeding
Blazing newer paths and fine;
When the force that is divine
Leaps to challenge every failure and his ardor still is sweet
And love and hope are burning in the presence of defeat …
Lo, the crisis! Lo, the shout
That must call the leader out.
When the people need salvation
Doth he come to lead the nation …
Then doth Nature show her plan
When the world has found—a man!

(From *Forward, March!* The John Lane Company, 1919)

I am convinced that failure is Nature's plan through which she hurdle-jumps men of destiny and prepares them to do their work. Failure is Nature's great crucible in which she burns the dross from the human heart and so purifies the metal of the man that it can stand the test of hard usage.

I have found evidence to support this theory in the study of the records of scores of great men, from Socrates and Christ on down the centuries to the well known men of achievement of our modern times. The success of each man seemed to be in almost exact ratio to the extent of the obstacles and difficulties he had to surmount.

No man ever arose from the knock-out blow of defeat without being stronger and wiser for the experience. Defeat talks to us in a language all its own; a language to which we must listen whether we like it or not.

Of course one must have considerable courage to look upon defeat as a blessing in disguise; but the attainment of any position in life, that is worth having requires a lot of "sand," which brings to mind a poem that harmonizes with the philosophy of this lesson.

If we could read the secret history of our enemies, we should find in each man's life sorrow and suffering enough to disarm all hostility.

–Longfellow

Sand

I observed a locomotive in the railroad yards one day,
It was waiting in the roundhouse where the locomotives stay;
It was panting for the journey, it was coaled and fully
    manned,
And it had a box the fireman was filling full of sand.

It appears that locomotives cannot always get a grip
On their slender iron pavement, 'cause the wheels are apt
    to slip;
And when they reach a slippery spot, their tactics they
    command,
And to get a grip upon the rail they sprinkle it with sand.

It's about the way with travel along life's slippery track,
If your load is rather heavy and you're always sliding back;
So if a common locomotive you completely understand,
You'll provide yourself in starting with a good supply of sand.

If your track is steep and hilly and you have a heavy grade,
If those who've gone before you have the rails quite
    slippery made,
If you ever reach the summit of the upper table land,
You'll find you'll have to do it with a liberal use of sand.

If you strike some frigid weather and discover, to your cost,
That you're liable to slip upon a heavy coat of frost,
Then some prompt, decided action will be called into demand,
And you'll slip 'way to the bottom if you haven't any sand.

You can get to any station that is on life's schedule seen
If there's fire beneath the boiler of ambition's strong
    machine,
And you'll reach a place called Flushtown at a rate of speed
    that's grand,
If for all the slippery places you've a good supply of sand.

It can do you no harm if you memorize the poems quoted in this
lesson and make the philosophy upon which they are based a part
of your own.

As I near the end of this lesson on Failure, there comes to mind a bit of philosophy taken from the works of the great Shakespeare, which I wish to challenge because I believe it to be unsound. It is stated in the following quotation:

There is a tide in the affairs of men
Which, taken at the flood, leads on to fortune;
Omitted, all the voyage of their life
Is bound in shallows, and in miseries.
On such a full sea are we now afloat;
And we must take the current when it serves,
Or lose our ventures.

Fear and admission of failure are the ties which cause us to be "bound in shallows, and in miseries." We can break these ties and throw them off. Nay, we can turn them to advantage and make them serve as a tow-line with which to pull ourselves ashore if we observe and profit by the lessons they teach.

Who ne'er has suffered, he has lived but half,
Who never failed, he never strove or sought,
Who never wept is stranger to a laugh,
And he who never doubted never thought.

As I near the end of this, my favorite lesson of this course, I close my eyes for a moment and see before me a great army of men and women whose faces show the lines of care and despair.

Some are in rags, having reached the last stage of that long, long trail which men call *failure!*

Others are in better circumstances, but the fear of starvation shows plainly on their faces; the smile of courage has left their lips; and they, too, seem to have given up the battle.

The scene shifts!

I look again and I am carried backward into the history of man's struggle for a place in the sun, and there I see, also, the "failures" of the past—failures that have meant more to the human race than all the so-called successes recorded in the history of the world.

I see the homely face of Socrates as he stood at the very end of that trail called failure, waiting, with upturned eyes, through those moments which must have seemed like an eternity, just before he drank the cup of hemlock that was forced upon him by his tormentors.

I see, also, Christopher Columbus, a prisoner in chains, which was the tribute paid him for his sacrifice in having set sail on an unknown and uncharted sea, to discover an unknown continent.

I see, also, the face of Thomas Paine, the man whom the English sought to capture and put to death as the real instigator of the American Revolution. I see him lying in a filthy prison, in France, as he waited calmly, under the shadow of the guillotine, for the death which he expected would be meted out to him for his part in behalf of humanity.

And I see, also, the face of the Man of Galilee, as he suffered on the cross of Calvary—the reward he received for his efforts in behalf of suffering humanity.

"Failures," all!

Tis the human touch in this world that counts,
The touch of your hand and mine,
Which means far more to the fainting heart
Than shelter and bread and wine;
For shelter is gone when the night is o'er,
And bread lasts only a day,
But the touch of the hand and the sound of the voice,
Sing on in the soul alway.

—Spencer M. Free

Oh, to be such a failure. Oh, to go down in history, as these men did, as one who was brave enough to place humanity above the individual and principle above pecuniary gain.

On such "failures" rest the hopes of the world.

> Oh, men, who are labeled "failures"—up, rise up! again and
>   do!
> Somewhere in the world of action is room; there is room
>   for you.
> No failure was e'er recorded, in the annals of truthful men,
> Except of the craven-hearted who fails, nor attempts again.
> The glory is in the doing, and not in the trophy won;
> The walls that are laid in darkness may laugh to the kiss of
>   the sun.
> Oh, weary and worn and stricken, oh, child of fate's cruel
>   gales!
> I sing—that it haply may cheer him—I sing to the man
>   who fails.

Be thankful for the defeat which men call failure, because if you can survive it and keep on trying it gives you a chance to prove your ability to rise to the heights of achievement in your chosen field of endeavor.

No one has the right to brand you as a failure except yourself.

If, in a moment of despair, you should feel inclined to brand yourself as a failure, just remember those words of the wealthy philosopher, Croesus, who was advisor to Cyrus, king of the Persians:

> I am reminded, O king, and take this lesson to heart, that there is a wheel on which the affairs of men revolve and its mechanism is such that it prevents *any* man from being *always* fortunate.

What a wonderful lesson is wrapped up in those words—a lesson of hope and courage and promise.

Who of us has not seen "off" days, when everything seemed to go wrong? These are the days when we see only the flat side of the great wheel of life.

Let us remember that the wheel is always turning. If it brings us sorrow today, it will bring us joy tomorrow. Life is a cycle of varying events—fortunes and misfortunes.

We cannot stop this wheel of fate from turning, but we can modify the misfortune it brings us by remembering that good fortune will follow, just as surely as night follows day, if we but keep faith with ourselves and earnestly and honestly do our best.

In his greatest hours of trial the immortal Lincoln was heard, often, to say: *"And this, too, will soon pass."*

If you are smarting from the effects of some temporary defeat which you find it hard to forget, let me recommend this stimulating little poem, by Walter Malone.

Opportunity

They do me wrong who say I come no more
  When once I knock and fail to find you in;
For every day I stand outside your door,
  And bid you wake, and rise to fight and win.

Wail not for precious chances passed away,
  Weep not for golden ages on the wane!
Each night I burn the records of the day—
  At sunrise every soul is born again!

Laugh like a boy at splendors that have sped,
  To vanished joys be blind and deaf and dumb;
My judgments seal the dead past with its dead,
  But never bind a moment yet to come.

Though deep in mire, wring not your hands and weep;
    I lend my arm to all who say "I can!"
No shame-faced outcast ever sank so deep,
    But yet might rise and be again a man!

Dost thou behold thy lost youth all aghast?
    Dost reel from righteous Retribution's blow?
Then turn from blotted archives of the past,
    And find the future's pages white as snow.

Art thou a mourner? Rouse thee from thy spell;
    Art thou a sinner? Sins may be forgiven;
Each morning gives thee wings to flee from hell,
    Each night a star to guide thy feet to heaven.

Strive not to banish pain and doubt,

In pleasure's noisy din;

The peace thou seekest from without,

Is only found within.

– Cary

Lesson 15
Tolerance

There are souls in this world which have the gift of finding joy everywhere, and of leaving it behind them everywhere they go.

– Faber

You Can Do It If You Believe You Can!

THERE ARE TWO significant features about intolerance, and your attention is directed to these at the beginning of this lesson.

These features are:

First: *Intolerance* is a form of ignorance which must be mastered before any form of enduring success may be attained. It is the chief cause of all wars. It makes enemies in business and in the professions. It disintegrates the organized forces of society in a thousand forms, and stands, like a mighty giant, as a barrier to the abolition of war. It dethrones reason and substitutes mob psychology in its place.

Second: Intolerance is the chief disintegrating force in the organized religions of the world, where it plays havoc with the greatest power for good there is on this earth; by breaking up that power into small sects and denominations which spend as much effort opposing each other as they do in destroying the evils of the world.

But this indictment against *intolerance* is general. Let's see how it affects you, the individual. It is, of course, obvious that anything which impedes the progress of civilization stands, also, as a barrier to each individual; and, stating it conversely, anything that beclouds the mind of the individual and retards his mental, moral and spiritual development, retards, also, the progress of civilization.

All of which is an abstract statement of a great truth; and, inasmuch as abstract statements are neither interesting nor highly informative, let us proceed to illustrate more concretely the damaging effects of *intolerance*.

I will begin this illustration by describing an incident which I have mentioned quite freely in practically every public address that I have delivered within the past five years; but, inasmuch as the cold printed page has a modifying effect which makes possible the misinterpretation of the incident here described, I believe it necessary to caution you not to read back of the lines a meaning which I had no intention of placing there. You will do yourself an injustice if you either neglect or intentionally refuse to study this illustration in the exact words and with the exact meaning which I have intended those words to convey—a meaning as clear as I know how to make the English language convey it.

As you read of this incident, place yourself in my position and see if you, also, have not had a parallel experience, and, if so, what lesson did it teach you?

One day I was introduced to a young man of unusually fine appearance. His clear eye, his warm handclasp, the tone of his voice and the splendid taste with which he was groomed marked him as a young man of the highest intellectual type. He was of the typical young American college student type, and as I ran my eyes over him, hurriedly studying his personality, as one will naturally do under such circumstances, I observed a Knights of Columbus pin on his vest.

Instantly, I released his hand as if it were a piece of ice!

This was done so quickly that it surprised both him and me. As I excused myself and started to walk away, I glanced down at the Masonic pin that I wore on my own vest, then took another look at his Knights of Columbus pin, and wondered why a couple of trinkets such as these could dig such a deep chasm between men who knew nothing of each other.

All the remainder of that day I kept thinking of the incident, because it bothered me. I had always taken considerable pride in the thought that I was tolerant with all men; but here was a spontaneous outburst of *intolerance* which proved that down in my subconscious mind existed a complex that was influencing me toward narrow-mindedness.

This discovery so shocked me that I began a systematic process of psycho-analysis through which I searched into the very depths of my soul for the cause of my rudeness.

I asked myself over and over again:

"Why did you abruptly release that young man's hand and turn away from him, when you knew nothing about him?"

Of course the answer led me, always, back to that Knights of Columbus pin that he wore. But that was not a real answer and therefore it did not satisfy me.

Then I began to do some research work in the field of religion. I began to study both Catholicism and Protestantism until I had traced both back to their beginning, a line of procedure which I must confess brought me more understanding of the problems of life than I had gathered from all other sources. For one thing it disclosed the fact that Catholicism and Protestantism differ more in *form* than they do in *effect*; that both are founded on exactly the same *cause*, which is Christianity.

But this was by no means all, nor was it the most important of my discoveries, for my research led, of necessity, in many directions, and forced me into the field of biology where I learned much that I needed to know about life in general and the human being in particular. My research led, also, to the study of Darwin's hypothesis of evolution, as outlined in his Origin of Species, and this, in turn, led to a much wider analysis of the subject of psychology than that which I had previously made.

As I began to reach out in this direction and that, for knowledge, my mind began to unfold and broaden with such alarming rapidity that I practically found it necessary to —

Wipe the slate of what I believed to be my previously gathered knowledge, and to unlearn much that I had previously believed to be truth.

Comprehend the meaning of that which I have just stated!

Imagine yourself suddenly discovering that most of your philosophy of life had been built of bias and prejudice, making it necessary for you to acknowledge that, far from being a finished scholar, *you were barely qualified to become an intelligent student!*

That was exactly the position in which I found myself, with respect to many of what I believed to be sound fundamentals of life; but of all the discoveries to which this research led, none was more important than that of the relative importance of *physical* and social heredity, for it was this discovery that disclosed the cause for my action when I turned away from a man whom I did not know, on the occasion that I have described.

It was this discovery that disclosed to me *how* and *where* I acquired my views of religion, of politics, of economics and many other equally important subjects, and I both regret and rejoice to state that *I found most of my views on these subjects without support by even a reasonable hypothesis,* much less sound facts or reason.

I then recalled a conversation between the late Senator Robert L. Taylor and myself, in which we were discussing the subject of

> *Hearts, like doors, can ope*
>
> *with ease,*
>
> *To very, very little keys;*
>
> *And don't forget that they*
>
> *are these:*
>
> *"I thank you, sir,"*
>
> *and "If you please."*

politics. It was a friendly discussion, as we were of the same political faith, but the Senator asked me a question for which I never forgave him until I began the research to which I have referred.

"I see that you are a very staunch Democrat," said he, "and I wonder if you know *why* you are?"

I thought of the question for a few seconds, then blurted out this reply:

"I am a Democrat because my father was one, of course!"

With a broad grin on his face the Senator then nailed me with this rejoinder:

"Just as I thought! Now wouldn't you be in a bad fix if your father had been a horse-thief?"

It was many years later, after I began the research work herein described, that I understood the real meaning of Senator Taylor's joke. Too often we hold opinions that are based upon no sounder foundation than that of what someone else believes.

That you may have a detailed illustration of the far-reaching effects of one of the important principles uncovered by the incident to which I have referred, and—

That you may learn how and where you acquired your philosophy of life, in general;

That you may trace your prejudices and your biases to their original source;

That you may discover, as I discovered, how largely you are the result of the training you received before you reached the age of fifteen years—

I will now quote the full text of a plan which I submitted to Mr. Edward Bok's Committee, The American Peace Award, for the abolition of war. This plan covers not only the most important of the principles to which I refer, but, as you will observe, it shows how the principle of *organized effort,* as outlined in Lesson Two of this course, may be applied to one of the most important of the world's problems, and at the same time gives you a more comprehensive idea of how to apply this principle in the *attainment* of *your definite chief aim.*

HOW TO ABOLISH WAR

The Background

Before offering this plan for the prevention of war, it seems necessary to sketch briefly a background that will clearly describe the principle which constitutes the warp and the woof of the plan.

The causes of war may be properly omitted for the reason that they have but little, if any, relation to the principle through which war may be prevented.

The beginning of this sketch deals with two important factors which constitute the chief controlling forces of civilization. One is *physical heredity* and the other is *social heredity.*

The size and form of the body, the texture of the skin, the color of the eyes, and the functioning power of the vital organs are all the result of physical heredity; they are static and fixed and cannot be changed, for they are the result of a million years of evolution; but by far the most important part of what we are is the result of social heredity, and came to us from the effects of our environment and early training.

Our conception of religion, politics, economics, philosophy and other subjects of a similar nature, including war, is entirely the result of those dominating forces of our environment and training.

The Catholic is a Catholic because of his early training and the Protestant is a Protestant for the same reason; but this is hardly stating the truth with sufficient emphasis, for it might be properly said that the Catholic is a Catholic and the Protestant is a Protestant *because he cannot help it!* With but few exceptions the religion of the adult is the result of his religious training during the years between four and fourteen when his religion was *forced* upon him by his parents or those who had control of his schooling.

A prominent clergyman indicated how well he understood the principle of social heredity when he said: "Give me the control of the child until it is twelve years old and you can teach it any religion you may please after that time, for I will have planted my own religion so deeply in its mind that no power on earth could undo my work."

The outstanding and most prominent of man's beliefs are those which were forced upon him, or which he absorbed of his own volition, under *highly emotionalized* conditions, when his mind was receptive. Under such conditions the evangelist can plant the idea of religion more deeply and permanently during an hour's revival service than he could through years of training under ordinary conditions, when the mind was not in an emotionalized state.

The people of the United States have immortalized Washington and Lincoln because they were the leaders of the nation during times when the minds of the people were highly emotionalized, as the result of calamities which shook the very foundation of our country and vitally affected the interests of all the people. Through the principle of social heredity, operating through the schools (American history), and through other forms of impressive teaching, the immortality of Washington and Lincoln is planted in the minds of the young and in that way kept alive.

The three great *organized forces* through which social heredity operates are:

The *schools,* the *churches* and the *public press.*

Any ideal that has the active co-operation of these three forces may, *during the brief period of one generation, be forced upon the minds of the young so effectively that they cannot resist it.*

In 1914 the world awoke one morning to find itself aflame with warfare on a scale previously unheard of, and the outstanding feature of importance of that world-wide calamity was the highly organized German armies. For more than three years these armies gained ground so rapidly that world domination by Germany seemed certain. The German military machine operated with efficiency such as had never before been demonstrated in warfare. With "kultur" as her avowed ideal, modern Germany swept the opposing armies before her as though they were leaderless, despite the fact that the allied forces outnumbered her own on every front.

The capacity for sacrifice in the German soldiers, in support of the ideal of "kultur," was the outstanding surprise of the war; and that capacity was largely the result of the work of two men. Through the German educational system, which they controlled, the psychology which carried the world into war in 1914 was created in the definite form of "kultur." These men were Adalbert Falk, Prussian Minister of Education until 1879, and the German Emperor William II.

The agency through which these men produced this result was *social heredity:* the imposing of an ideal on the minds of the young, under highly emotionalized conditions.

"Kultur," as a national ideal, was fixed in the minds of the young of Germany, beginning first in the elementary schools and extending on up through the high schools and universities. *The teachers and professors were forced to implant the ideal of "kultur" in the minds of the students,* and out of this teaching, in a single generation, grew the capacity for sacrifice of the individual for the interest of the nation which surprised the modern world.

As Benjamin Kidd so well stated the case: "The aim of the state of Germany was everywhere to orientate public opinion through the heads of both its spiritual and temporal departments, through the bureaucracy, through the officers of the army, through the State direction of the press; and, last of all, through the State direction of the entire trade and industry of the nation, so as to bring the idealism of the whole people to a conception of and to a support of the national policy of modern Germany."

Germany controlled the press, the clergy and the schools; therefore, is it any wonder that she grew an army of soldiers, during one generation, which represented to a man her ideal of "kultur"? Is it any wonder that the German soldiers faced certain death with fearless impunity, when one stops to consider the fact that they had been taught, from early childhood, that this sacrifice was a rare privilege?

Turn, now, from this brief description of the modus operandi through which Germany prepared her people for war, to another strange phenomenon, Japan. No western nation, with the exception of Germany, has so clearly manifested its understanding of the far-reaching influence of social heredity, as has Japan. Within a single generation Japan has advanced from her standing as a fourth-rate nation to the ranks of nations that are the recognized powers of the civilized world. Study Japan and you will find that she forces upon the minds of her young, through exactly the same agencies employed by Germany, the ideal of subordination of individual rights for the sake of accumulation of power by the nation.

It takes but a second to administer a rebuke, but it may take a life-time for the one who has been rebuked to forget it.

In all of her controversies with China, competent observers have seen that back of the apparent causes of the controversies was Japan's stealthy attempt to control the minds of the young by controlling the schools. *If Japan could control the minds of the young of China, she could dominate that gigantic nation within one generation.*

If you would study the effect of social heredity as it is being used for the development of a national ideal by still another nation of the West, observe what has been going on in Russia since the ascendency to power of the soviet government of Russia which is now patterning the minds of the young to conform with a national ideal, the nature of which it requires no master analyst to interpret. That ideal, when fully developed during the maturity of the present generation, will represent exactly that which the soviet government wishes it to represent.

Of all the flood of propaganda concerning the soviet government of Russia that has been poured into this country through the tens of thousands of columns of newspaper space devoted to it since the close of the war, the following brief dispatch is by far the most significant:

Russ Reds Order Books

*Contracts being let in Germany for 20,000,000 volumes.
Educational propaganda is aimed chiefly at children.*

By George Witts
Special Cable to the Chicago Daily News Foreign Service
Berlin, Germany, November 9th, 1920.

Contracts for printing 20,000,000 books *in the Russian language,* chiefly for children, are being placed in Germany on behalf of the soviet government by Grschebin, a well known Petrograd publisher and a friend of Maxim Gorky. Grschebin first went to England, but was received with indifference when he broached the subject to the British government. *The Germans, however, not only welcomed him eagerly but submitted prices so low that they could not possibly be underbidden in any other country.* The Ullsteins, Berlin newspaper and book publishers, have agreed to print several million of the books at less than cost.

This shows what is going on over there.

Far from being shocked by this significant press dispatch, the majority of the newspapers of America did not publish it, and those that did give it space placed it in an obscure part of the paper, in small type. Its real significance will become more apparent some twenty-odd years from now, when the soviet government of Russia will have grown an army of soldiers who will support, to the man, *whatever national ideal the soviet government sets up.*

The possibility of war exists as a stern reality today solely because the principle of social heredity has not only been used as a sanctioning force in support of war, but it has actually been used as a chief agency through which the minds of men have been deliberately prepared for war. For evidence with which to support this statement, examine any national or world history and *observe how tactfully and effectively war has been glorified and so described that it not only did not shock the mind of the student, but it actually established a plausible justification of war.*

Go into the public squares of our cities and observe the monuments that have been erected to the leaders of war. Observe the posture of these statues as they stand as living symbols to glorify men who did nothing more than lead armies on escapades of destruction. Notice how well these statues of warriors, mounted on charging steeds, serve as agencies through which to stimulate the minds of the young and prepare them for the acceptance of war, not only as a pardonable act, but as a distinctly desirable source of attainment of glory, fame and honor. At the time of this writing some well meaning ladies are having the image of Confederate Soldiers carved in the deathless granite on the face of Stone Mountain, in Georgia, in figures a hundred feet tall, thus seeking to perpetuate the memory of a lost "cause" that never was a "cause" and therefore the sooner forgotten, the better.

If these references to far-away Russia, Japan and Germany seem unimpressive and abstract, then let us study the principle of social heredity as it is now functioning on a highly developed scale here in the United States; for it may be expecting too much of the average of our race to suppose that they will be interested in that which is taking place outside of the spot of ground that is bounded on the north by Canada, on the east by the Atlantic, on the west by the Pacific and on the south by Mexico.

We, too, are setting up in the minds of our young a national ideal, and this ideal is being so effectively developed, through the principle of social heredity, that it has already become the dominating ideal of the nation.

This ideal is the desire for wealth!

The first question we ask about a new acquaintance is not, "Who are you?" but, "What have you?" And the next question we ask is, *"How can we get that which you have?"*

Our ideal is not measured in terms of warfare, but in terms of finance and industry and business. Our Patrick Henrys and our George Washingtons and our Abraham Lincolns of a few generations ago are now represented by the able leaders who manage our steel mills and our coal mines and our timber lands and our banking institutions and our railroads.

We may deny this indictment if we choose, but the facts do not support the denial.

Unfortunate, indeed, is the man who becomes so used to evil that it no longer appears to be horrible.

The outstanding problem of the American people today is the spirit of unrest upon the part of the masses who find the struggle for existence becoming harder and harder because the most competent brains of the country are engaged in the highly competitive attempt to accumulate wealth and to control the wealth-producing machinery of the nation.

It is not necessary to dwell at length upon this description of our dominating ideal, or to offer evidence in support of its existence, for the reason that its existence is obvious and as well understood by the most ignorant as it is by those who make a pretense of thinking accurately.

So deeply seated has this mad desire for money become that we are perfectly willing for the other nations of the world to cut themselves to pieces in warfare so long as they do not interfere with our scramble for wealth; nor is this the saddest part of the indictment that we might render against ourselves, for we are not only *willing* for other nations to engage in warfare, but there is considerable reason to believe that those of us who profit by the sale of war supplies actually encourage this warfare among other nations.

The Plan

War grows out of the desire of the individual to gain advantage at the expense of his fellow men, and the smoldering embers of this desire are fanned into a flame through the grouping of these individuals who place the interests of the group above those of other groups.

War cannot be stopped suddenly!

It can be eliminated only by education, through the aid of the principle of subordination of the individual interests to the broader interests of the human race as a whole.

Man's tendencies and activities, as we have already stated, grow out of two great forces. One is *physical* heredity, and the other is *social* heredity. Through physical heredity, man inherits those early tendencies to destroy his fellow man out of self-protection. This practice is a hold-over from prehistory when the struggle for existence was so great that only the physically strong could survive.

Gradually man began to learn that the individual could survive under more favorable circumstances by allying himself with others, and out of that discovery grew our modern society, through which groups of people have formed states, and these groups, in turn, have formed nations, There is but little tendency toward warfare between the individuals of a particular group or nation, for they have learned, through the principle of *social* heredity, that they can best survive by subordinating the interest of the individual to that of the group.

Now, the problem is to extend this principle of grouping so that *the nations of the world will subordinate their individual interests to those of the human race as a whole.*

This can be brought about only through the principle of social heredity. *By forcing upon the minds of the young of all races the fact that war is horrible and does not serve either the interest of the individual engaging in it or the group to which the individual belongs.*

The question then arises, "How can this be done?" Before we answer this question, let us again define the term *"social heredity"* and find out what its possibilities are.

Social heredity is the principle through which the young of the race absorb from their environment, and particularly from their earlier training by parents, teachers and religious leaders, *the beliefs and tendencies of the adults who dominate them.*

Any plan to abolish war, to be successful, depends upon the successful co-ordination of effort between *all the churches and schools of the world for the avowed purpose of so fertilizing the minds of the young with the idea of abolishing war that the very word "war" will strike terror in their hearts.*

THERE IS NO OTHER WAY OF ABOLISHING WAR!

The next question that arises, "How can the churches and schools of the world be organized with this high ideal as an objective?" The answer is that not all of them can be induced to enter into such an alliance, at one time; but a sufficient number of the more influential ones can be induced, and this, in time, will lead or *force* the remainder into the alliance, as rapidly as public opinion begins to *demand it.*

Then comes the question, "Who has sufficient influence to call a conference of the most powerful religious and educational leaders?" The answer is:

The President and Congress of the United States.

Such an undertaking would *command* the support of the press on a scale heretofore unheard of, and through this source alone the propaganda would begin to reach and fertilize the minds of the people in every civilized country in the world, in preparation for the adoption of the plan in the churches and schools throughout the world.

The plan for the abolition of war might be likened to a great dramatic play, with these as the chief factors:

STAGE SETTING: At the Capitol of the United States.

STAR ACTORS: The President and members of Congress.

MINOR ACTORS: The leading clergymen of all denominations, and the leading educators, all on the stage by invitation and at the expense of the United States government.

PRESS ROOM: Representatives of the news-gathering agencies
of the world.

STAGE EQUIPMENT: A radio broadcasting outfit that would
distribute the entire proceedings halfway round the earth.

TITLE OF THE PLAY: "Thou shalt not kill!"

OBJECT OF THE PLAY: The creation of a World Court, to be
made up of representatives of all races, whose duty it would
be to hear evidence and adjudicate the cases arising out of
disagreement between nations.

Other factors would enter into this great world drama, but they
would be of minor importance. The main issues and the most essential factors are here enumerated.

One other question remains, "Who will start the machinery of
the United States government into action to call this conference?"
and the answer is:

*Public opinion, through the aid of an able organizer and leader, who
will organize and direct the efforts of a Golden Rule Society, the object of
which will be to move the President and Congress into action.*

No League of Nations and no mere agreement between nations
can abolish war as long as there is the slightest evidence of sanction of
war in the hearts of the people. Universal peace between nations will
grow out of a movement that will be begun and carried on, at first, by
a comparatively small number of thinkers. Gradually this number will
grow until it will be composed of the leading educators, clergymen
and publicists of the world, and these, in turn, will so deeply and permanently establish *peace* as a world ideal that it will become a reality.

This desirable end may be attained in a single generation under
the right sort of leadership; but, more likely, it will not be attained
for many generations to come, for the reason that those who have
the ability to assume this leadership are too busy in their pursuit of
worldly wealth to make the necessary sacrifice for the good of generations yet unborn.

War can be eliminated, not by appeal to reason, but by appeal to the emotional side of humanity. This appeal must be made by *organizing and highly emotionalizing the people of the different nations of the world in support of a universal plan for peace, and this plan must be forced upon the minds of the oncoming generations with the same diligent care that we now force upon the minds of our young the ideal of our respective religions.*

It is not stating the possibilities too strongly to say that the churches of the world could establish universal peace as an international ideal within one generation if they would but *direct toward that end one-half of the effort which they now employ in opposing one another.*

We would still be within the bounds of conservatism if we stated that the Christian churches, alone, have sufficient influence to establish universal peace as a world-wide ideal, within three generations, if the various sects would combine their forces for the purpose.

That which the leading churches of all religions, the leading schools and the public press of the world could accomplish in forcing the ideal of universal peace upon *both the adult and the child mind of the world* within a single generation, staggers the imagination.

If the organized religions of the world, as they now exist, will not subordinate their individual interests and purposes to that of establishing universal peace, then the remedy lies in establishing a universal church of the world that will function through all races and whose creed will be based entirely upon the one purpose of implanting in the minds of the young the ideal of world-wide peace.

Such a church would gradually attract a following from the rank and file of all other churches.

And if the educational institutions of the world will not co-operate in fostering this high ideal of universal peace, then the remedy lies in the creation of an entirely new educational system that will implant in the minds of the young the ideal of universal peace.

And if the public press of the world will not cooperate in setting up the ideal of universal peace, then the remedy lies in the creation of an independent press that will utilize both the printed page and the forces of the air for the purpose of creating mass support of this high ideal.

In brief, if the present *organized forces* of the world will not lend their support to establishing universal peace, as an international ideal, then new organizations must be created which will do so.

The majority of the people of the world want peace, wherein lies the possibility of its attainment!

At first thought, it seems too much to expect that the organized churches of the world can be induced to pool their power and subordinate their individual interests to those of civilization as a whole.

But this seemingly insurmountable obstacle is, in reality, no obstacle at all, for the reason that whatever support this plan borrows from the churches it gives back to them, a thousand fold, through the increased power the church attains.

Let us see just what advantages the church realizes by participation in this plan to establish *universal peace* as a world ideal. First of all, it

> *Greatly begin! though*
> *though have time,*
> *But for a line, be that*
> *sublime —*
> *Not failure, but low*
> *aim is crime.*

will be clearly seen that no individual church loses any of its advantages by allying itself with other denominations in establishing this world ideal. The alliance in no way changes or interferes with the creed of any church. Every church entering the alliance will come out of it with all the power and advantages that it possessed before it went in, plus the additional advantage of greater influence which the church, as a whole, will enjoy by reason of having served as the leading factor in forcing upon civilization the greatest single benefit it has enjoyed in the history of the world.

If the church gained no other advantages from the alliance, this one would be sufficient to compensate it. *But the important advantage that the church will have gained by this alliance is the discovery that it has sufficient power to force its ideals upon the world when it places its combined support back of the undertaking.*

By this alliance the church will have grasped the far-reaching significance of the principle of *organized effort* through the aid of which it might easily have dominated the world and imposed its ideals upon civilization.

The church is by far the greatest potential power in the world today, but its power is merely potential and will remain so until it makes use of the principle of allied or *organized* effort; that is to say, until *all denominations formulate a working agreement under which the combined strength of organized religion will be used as a means of forcing a higher ideal upon the minds of the young.*

The reason that the church is the greatest potential power in the world is the fact that its power grows out of man's emotions. *Emotion rules the world, and the church is the only organization which rests solely upon the power of emotion. The church is the only organized factor of society which has the power to harness and direct the emotional forces of civilization, for the reason that the emotions are controlled by* FAITH *and not by reason! And the church is the only great organized body in which faith of the world is centered.*

The church stands today as so many disconnected units of power, and it is not overstating the possibilities to say that when these units shall have been connected, *through allied effort,* the combined power of that alliance *will rule the world and there is no opposing power on earth that can defeat it!*

It is in no discouraging spirit that this statement is followed by another which may seem still more radical; namely:

The task of bringing about this alliance of the churches in support of the world ideal of universal peace must rest upon the female members of the church, for the reason that the abolition of war promises advantages that may be prolonged into the future and that may accrue only to the unborn generations.

In Schopenhauer's bitter arraignment of woman, he unconsciously stated a truth upon which the hope of civilization rests, when he declared that *the race is always to her more than the individual.* In terms that are uncompromising, Schopenhauer charges woman with being the natural enemy of man because of this inborn trait *of placing the interests of the race above those of the individual.*

It seems a reasonable prophecy to suggest that civilization passed into a new era, beginning with the world war, in which woman is destined to take into her own hands the raising of the ethical standards of the world. This is a hopeful sign, because it is woman's nature to subordinate the interests of the present to those of the future. It is woman's nature to implant, in the mind of the young, ideals that will accrue to the benefit of generations yet unborn, while man is motivated generally by expediency of the present.

In Schopenhauer's vicious attack upon woman, he has stated a great truth concerning her nature: a truth which might well be utilized by all who engage in the worthy work of establishing *universal peace as a world ideal.*

The women's clubs of the world are destined to play a part in world affairs other than that of gaining suffrage for women.

LET CIVILIZATION REMEMBER THIS!

Those who do not want peace are the ones who profit by war. In numbers, this class constitutes but a fragment of the power of the world, and could be swept aside as though it did not exist, if the multitude who do not want war were organized with the high ideal of universal peace as their objective.

In closing, it seems appropriate to apologize for the unfinished state of this essay, but it may be pardonable to suggest that the bricks and the mortar, and the foundation stones, and all the other necessary materials for the construction of the *temple of universal peace* have been here assembled, where they might be re-arranged and transformed into this high ideal as a world reality.

Let us now proceed to apply the principle of *social heredity* to the subject of business economy, and ascertain whether or not it can be made of practical benefit in the attainment of material wealth.

If I were a banker I would procure a list of all the births in the families within a given distance of my place of business, and every child would receive an appropriate letter, congratulating it on its arrival in the world at such an opportune time, in such a favorable community; and from that time on it would receive from my bank a birthday reminder of an appropriate nature. When it arrived at the story-book age, it would receive from my bank an interesting story book in which the advantages of saving would be told in story form. If the child were a girl, it would receive doll "cut-out" books, with the name of my bank on the back of each doll, as a birthday gift. If it were a boy, it would receive baseball bats. One of the most important floors (or even a whole, near-by building) of my banking house would be set aside as a children's play-room; and it would be equipped with merry-go-rounds, sliding-boards, seesaws, scooters, games and sand piles, with a competent supervisor in charge to give the kiddies a good time. I would let that play-room become the popular habitat of the children of the community, where mothers might leave their youngsters in safety while shopping or visiting.

I would entertain those youngsters so royally that when they grew up and became bank depositors, whose accounts were worth while, they would be inseparably bound to my bank; and, meanwhile, I would, in no way, be lessening my chances of making depositors of the fathers and mothers of those children.

If I were the owner of a business school, I would begin cultivating the boys and girls of my community from the time they reached the fifth grade, on up through high school, so that by the time they were through high school and ready to choose a vocation, I would have the name of my business school well fixed in their minds.

If I were a grocer, or a department store owner, or a druggist, I would cultivate the children, thereby attracting both them and their parents to my place of business; for it is a well known fact that there is no shorter route to the heart of a parent than that which leads through interest manifested in the offspring. If I were a department store owner, and used whole pages of newspaper space, as most of them do, I would run a comic strip at the bottom of each page, illustrating it with scenes in my play-room, and in this way induce the children to read my advertisements.

If I were a preacher, I would equip the basement of my church with a children's play-room that would attract the children of the community every day in the week; and, if my study were near by, I would go into that play-room and enjoy the fun with the little fellows, thereby gaining the inspiration with which to preach better sermons while at the same time raising parishioners for tomorrow. I can think of no more effective method than this of rendering a service that would be in harmony with Christianity, and which would, at the same time, make my church a popular place of abode for the young folks.

If I were a national advertiser, or the owner of a mail order house, I would find appropriate ways and means of establishing a point of contact with the children of the country; for, let me repeat, there is no better way of influencing the parent than that of "capturing" the child.

If I were a barber, I would have a room equipped exclusively for children, for this would bring me the patronage of both the children and their parents.

In the outskirts of every city there is an opportunity for a flourishing business for someone who will operate a restaurant and serve meals of the better "home-cooked" quality, and cater to families who wish to take the children and dine out occasionally. I would have the place equipped with well stocked fishing ponds, and ponies, and all sorts of animals and birds in which children are interested, if I were operating it, and induce the children to come out regularly and spend the entire day. Why speak of gold mines when opportunities such as this are abundant?

These are but a few of the ways in which the principle of *social heredity* might be used to advantage in business,

Attract the children and you attract the parents!

If nations can build soldiers of war to order, by bending the minds of their young in the direction of war, business men can build customers to order through the same principle.

We come, now, to another important feature of this lesson through which we may see, from another angle, how power may be accumulated by co-operative, *organized effort.*

In the plan for the abolition of war, you observed how co-ordination of effort between three of the great organized powers of the world (the schools, churches and the public press) might serve to force universal peace.

We learned many lessons of value from the world war, outrageous and destructive as it was, but none of greater importance than that of the effect of *organized effort*. You will recall that the tide of war began to break in favor of the allied armies just after all armed forces were placed under the direction of General Foch, which brought about complete co-ordination of effort in the allied ranks.

Never before, in the history of the world, had so much power been concentrated in one group of men as that which was created through the *organized effort* of the allied armies. We come, now, to one of the most outstanding and significant facts to be found in the analysis of these allied armies, namely, that they were made up of the most cosmopolitan group of soldiers ever assembled on this earth.

Catholics and Protestants, Jews and Gentiles, blacks and whites, yellows and tans, and every race on earth were represented in those armies. If they had any differences on account of race or creed, they laid them aside and subordinated them to the *cause* for which they were fighting. Under the stress of war, that great mass of humanity was reduced to a common level where they fought shoulder to shoulder, side by side, without asking any questions as to each other's racial tendencies or religious beliefs.

If they could lay aside *intolerance* long enough to fight for their lives over there, why can we not do the same while we fight for a higher standard of ethics in business and finance and industry over here?

Is it only when civilized people are fighting for their lives that they have the foresight to lay aside *intolerance* and co-operate in the furtherance of a common end?

If it were advantageous to the allied armies to think and act as one thoroughly co-ordinated body, would it be less advantageous for the people of a city or a community or an industry to do so?

If all the churches and schools and newspapers and clubs and civic organizations of your city allied themselves for the further-ance of a common cause, do you not see how such an alliance would create sufficient power to insure the success of that cause?

Bring the illustration still nearer your own individual interests by an imaginary alliance between all of the employers and all of the employees of your city, for the purpose of reducing friction and mis-understandings, thereby enabling them to render better service at a lower cost to the public and greater profit to themselves.

We learned from the world war that we cannot destroy a part without weakening the whole; that when one nation or group of people is reduced to poverty and want, the remainder of the world suffers, also. Stated conversely, we learned from the world war that *co-operation* and *tolerance* are the very foundation of enduring success.

Surely the more thoughtful and observant individuals will not fail to profit (as individuals) by these great lessons which we learned from the world war.

I am not unmindful of the fact that *you* are probably study-ing this course for the purpose of profiting, in every way possible, from a purely personal viewpoint, by the principles upon which it is founded. For this very reason, I have endeavored to outline the ap-plication of these principles to as wide a scope of subjects as possible.

In this lesson, you have had opportunity to observe the appli-cation of the principles underlying the subjects of *organized effort, tolerance* and *social heredity* to an extent which must have given you much food for thought, and which must have given your imagination much room for profitable exercise.

I have endeavored to show you how these principles may be employed both in the furtherance of your own individual interests, in whatever calling you may be engaged, and for the benefit of civilization as a whole.

Whether your calling is that of preaching sermons, selling goods or personal services, practicing law, directing the efforts of others, or working as a day laborer, it seems not too much to hope that you will find in this lesson a stimulus to thought which may lead you to higher achievements. If, perchance, you are a writer of advertisements you will surely find in this lesson sufficient food for thought to add more power to your pen. If you have personal services for sale, it is not unreasonable to expect that this lesson will suggest ways and means of marketing those services to greater advantage.

In uncovering for you the source from which intolerance is usually developed, this lesson has led you, also, to the study of other thought-provoking subjects which might easily mark the most profitable turning-point of your life. Books and lessons, in themselves, are of but little value; their real value, if any, lies not in their printed pages, *but in the possible action which they may arouse in the reader.*

For example, when my proof-reader had finished reading the manuscript of this lesson, she informed me that it had so impressed her and her husband that they intended to go into the advertising business and supply banks with an advertising service that would reach the parents through the children. She believes the plan is worth $10,000.00 a year to her.

Frankly, her plan so appealed to me that I would estimate its value at a minimum of more than three times the amount she mentioned, and I doubt not that it could be made to yield five times that amount, if it were properly organized and marketed by an able salesman.

Nor is that all that this lesson has accomplished before passing from the manuscript stage. A prominent business college owner, to whom I showed the manuscript, has already begun to put into effect the suggestion which referred to the use of *social heredity* as a means of "cultivating" students; and he is sanguine enough to believe that a plan, similar to the one he intends using, could be sold to the majority of the 1500 business colleges in the United States and Canada, on a basis that would yield the promoter of the plan a yearly income greater than the salary received by the President of the United States.

And, as this lesson is being completed, I am in receipt of a letter from Dr. Charles F. Crouch, of Atlanta, Georgia, in which he informs me that a group of prominent business men in Atlanta have just organized the Golden Rule Club, the main object of which is to put into operation, on a nation-wide scale, the plan for the abolition of war, as outlined in this lesson. (A copy of that portion of this lesson dealing with the subject of abolition of war was sent to Dr. Crouch several weeks before the completion of the lesson.)

> *If a man has built a sound character it makes but little difference what people say about him, because he will win in the end.*
>
> *–Napoleon Hill, Sr.*

These three events, happening one after the other, within a period of a few weeks, have strengthened my belief that this is the most important lesson of the entire sixteen, but its value to *you* will depend entirely upon the extent to which it stimulates you to *think* and to *act* as you would not have done without its influence.

The chief object of this course and, particularly, of this lesson is to *educate*, more than it is to *inform*—meaning by the word "educate" to educe, to draw out! to develop from within; *to cause you to use the power that lies sleeping within you, awaiting the awakening hand of some appropriate stimulus to arouse you to action.*

In conclusion, may I not leave with you my personal sentiments on tolerance, in the following essay which I wrote, in the hour of my most trying experience, when an enemy was trying to ruin my reputation and destroy the results of a life-time of honest effort to do some good in the world.

TOLERANCE!

When the dawn of Intelligence shall have spread its wings over the eastern horizon of progress, and ignorance and Superstition shall have left their last footprints on the sands of Time, it will be recorded in the book of man's crimes and mistakes that his most grievous sin was that of Intolerance!

The bitterest Intolerance grows out of racial and religious differences of opinion, as the result of early childhood training. How long, O Master of Human Destinies, until we poor mortals will understand the folly of trying to destroy one another because of dogmas and creeds and other superficial matters over which we do not agree?

Our allotted time on this earth is but a fleeting moment, at most!

Like a candle, we are lighted, shine for a moment and flicker out! Why can we not so live during this short earthly sojourn that when the Great Caravan called Death draws up and announces this visit about finished we will be ready to fold our tents, and, like the Arabs of the Desert, silently follow the Caravan out into the Darkness of the Unknown without fear and trembling?

I am hoping that I will find no Jews or Gentiles, Catholics or Protestants, Germans or Englishmen, Frenchmen or Russians, Blacks or Whites, Reds or Yellows, when I shall have crossed the Bar to the Other Side.

I am hoping I will find there only human Souls, Brothers and Sisters all, unmarked by race, creed or color, for I shall want to be done with Intolerance so I may lie down and rest an one or two, undisturbed by the strife, ignorance, superstition and petty misunderstandings which mark with chaos and grief this earthly existence.

LESSON 16
THE GOLDEN RULE

No man could possibly read the Law of Success

philosophy, even once, without becoming, thereby,

better prepared to succeed in any calling.

–Elbert H. Gary

You Can Do It If You Believe You Can!

WITH THIS LESSON we approach the apex of the pyramid of this course on the Law of Success.

This lesson is the Guiding Star that will enable you to use profitably and *constructively* the knowledge assembled in the preceding lessons.

There is more power wrapped up in the preceding lessons of this course than most men could trust themselves with; therefore, this lesson is a governor that will, if observed and applied, enable you to steer your ship of knowledge over the rocks and reefs of failure that usually beset the pathway of all who come suddenly into possession of power.

For more than twenty-five years I have been observing the manner in which men behave themselves when in possession of power, and I have been forced to the conclusion that the man who attains it in any other than by the slow, step-by-step process, is constantly in danger of destroying himself and all whom he influences.

It must have become obvious to you, long before this, that this entire course leads to the attainment of *power* of proportions which may be made to perform the seemingly "impossible." Happily, it becomes apparent that this power can only be attained by the observance of many fundamental principles all of which converge in this lesson, which is based upon a law that both equals and transcends in importance every other law outlined in the preceding lessons.

Likewise, it becomes apparent to the thoughtful student that this *power* can endure only by faithful observance of the law upon which this lesson is based, wherein lies the "safety-valve" that protects the careless student from the dangers of his own follies; and protects, also, those who-n he might endanger if he tried to circumvent the injunction laid down in this lesson.

To "prank" with the power that may be attained from the knowledge wrapped up in the preceding lessons of this course, without a full understanding and strict observance of the law laid down in this lesson, is the equivalent of "pranking" with a power which may destroy as well as create.

I am speaking, now, not of that which I suspect to be true, but, of that which I KNOW TO BE TRUE! The truth upon which this entire course, and this lesson in particular, is founded, is no invention of mine. I lay no claim to it except that of having observed its unvarying application in the every-day walks of life over a period of more than twenty-five years of struggle; and, of having appropriated as much of it as, in the light of my human frailties and weaknesses, I could make use of.

If you demand *positive* proof of the soundness of the laws upon which this course in general, and this lesson in particular, is founded, I must plead inability to offer it except through one witness, and that is *yourself.*

You may have *positive* proof only by testing and applying these laws for yourself.

If you demand more substantial and authoritative evidence than my own, then I am privileged to refer you to the teachings and philosophy of Christ, Plato, Socrates, Epictetus, Confucius, Emerson and two of the more modern philosophers, James and Münsterberg, from whose works I have appropriated all that constitutes the more important fundamentals of this lesson, with the exception of that which I have gathered from my own limited experience.

For more than four thousand years men have been preaching the Golden Rule as a suitable rule of conduct among men, but unfortunately the world has accepted the letter while totally missing the spirit of this Universal Injunction. We have accepted the Golden Rule philosophy merely as a sound rule of ethical conduct but we have failed to understand the law upon which it is based.

I have heard the Golden Rule quoted scores of times, but I do not recall having ever heard an explanation of the law upon which it is based, and not until recent years did I understand that law, from which am led to believe that those who quoted it did not understand it.

The Golden Rule means, substantially, to do unto others as you would wish them to do unto you if your positions were reversed.

But why? What is the *real* reason for this kindly consideration of others?

The real reason is this:

There is an eternal law through the operation of which we reap that which we sow. When you select the rule of conduct by which you guide yourself in your transactions with others, you will be fair and just, very likely, if you know that you are setting into motion, by that selection, a *power* that will run its course for weal or woe in the lives of others, returning, finally, to help or to hinder you, according to its nature.

"Whatsoever a man soweth that shall he also reap!"

It is your privilege to deal unjustly with others, but, if you understand the law upon which the Golden Rule is based, you must know that your unjust dealings will "come home to roost."

If you fully understood the principles described in Lesson Eleven, on *accurate thought,* it will be quite easy for you to understand the law upon which the Golden Rule is based. You cannot pervert or change the course of this law, *but you can adapt yourself to its nature and thereby use it as an irresistible power that will carry you to heights of achievement which could not be attained without its aid.*

This law does not stop by merely flinging back upon you your acts of injustice and unkindness toward others; it goes further than this—much further—and returns to you the results of every *thought* that you release.

Therefore, not alone is it advisable to "do unto others as you wish them to do unto you," but to avail yourself fully of the benefits of this great Universal Law you must "think of others as you wish them to think of you."

The law upon which the Golden Rule is based begins affecting you, either for good or evil, the moment you release a *thought*. It has amounted almost to a world-wide tragedy that people have not generally understood this law. Despite the simplicity of the law it is practically all there is to be learned that is of enduring value to man, for it is the medium through which we become the masters of our own destiny.

Understand this law and you understand *all* that the Bible has to unfold to you, for the Bible presents one unbroken chain of evidence in support of the fact that man is the maker of his own destiny; and, that his *thoughts* and *acts* are the tools with which he does the *making*.

During ages of less enlightenment and tolerance than that of the present, some of the greatest thinkers the world has ever pro-duced have paid with their lives for daring to uncover this Universal Law so that it might be understood by all. In the light of the past history of the world, it is an encouraging bit of evidence, in support of the fact that men are gradually throwing off the veil of ignorance and intolerance, to note that I stand in no danger of bodily harm for writing that which would have cost me my life a few centuries ago.

While this course deals with the highest laws of the universe, which man is capable of interpreting, the aim, nevertheless, has been to show how these laws may be used in the practical affairs of life. With this object of practical application in mind, let us now proceed to analyze the effect of the Golden Rule through the following incident.

THE POWER OF PRAYER

"No," said the lawyer, "I shan't press your claim against that man; you can get someone else to take the case, or you can withdraw it; just as you please."

"Think there isn't any money in it?"

"There probably would be some little money in it, but it would come from the sale of the little house that the man occupies and calls his home! But I don't want to meddle with the matter, anyhow."

"Got frightened out of it, eh?"

"Not at all."

"I suppose likely the fellow begged hard to be let off?"

"Well, yes, he did."

"And you caved in, likely?"

"Yes."

"What in creation did you do?"

"I believe I shed a few tears."

"And the old fellow begged you hard, you say?"

"No, I didn't say so; he didn't speak a word to me."

"Well, may I respectfully inquire whom he did address in your hearing?"

"God Almighty."

"Ah, he took to praying, did he?"

"Not for my benefit, in the least. You see, I found the little house easily enough and knocked on the outer door, which stood ajar; but nobody heard me, so I stepped into the little hall and saw through the crack of a door a cozy sitting-room, and there on the bed, with her silver head high on the pillows, was an old lady who looked for all the world just like my mother did the last time I ever saw her on earth. Well, I was on the point of knocking, when she said: 'Come, father, now begin; I'm all ready.' And down on his knees by her side went an old, white-haired man, still older than his wife, I should judge, and I couldn't have knocked then, for the life of me. Well, he began.

First, he reminded God they were still His submissive children, mother and he, and no matter what He saw fit to bring upon them they shouldn't rebel at His will. Of course 'twas going to be very hard for them to go out homeless in their old age, especially with poor mother so sick and helpless, and, oh! how different it all might have been if only one of the boys had been spared. Then his voice kind of broke, and a white hand stole from under the coverlid and moved softly over his snowy hair. Then he went on to repeat that nothing could be so sharp again as the parting with those three sons—unless mother and he should be separated.

Every man takes care that his neighbor does not cheat him. But a day comes when he begins to care that he does not cheat his neighbor. Then all goes well. He has changed his market cart into a chariot of the sun.

"But, at last, he fell to comforting himself with the fact that the dear Lord knew that it was through no fault of his own that mother and he were threatened with the loss of their dear little home, which meant beggary and the alms-house—a place they prayed to be delivered from entering if it should be consistent with God's will. And then he quoted a multitude of promises concerning the safety of those who put their trust in the Lord. In fact, it was the most thrilling plea to which I ever listened. And at last, he prayed for God's blessing on those who were about to demand justice."

The lawyer then continued, more lowly than ever: "And I—believe—I'd rather go to the poor-house myself tonight than to stain my heart and hands with the blood of such a prosecution as that."

"Little afraid to defeat the old man's prayer, eh?"

"Bless your soul, man, you couldn't defeat it!" said the lawyer. "I tell you he left it all subject to the will of God; but he claimed that we were told to make known our desires unto God; but of all the pleadings I ever heard that beat all. You see, I was taught that kind of thing myself in my childhood. Anyway, why was I sent to hear that prayer? I am sure I don't know, but I hand the case over."

"I wish," said the client, twisting uneasily, "you hadn't told me about the old man's prayer."

"Why so?"

"Well, because I want the money the place would bring; but I was taught the Bible straight enough when I was a youngster and I'd hate to run counter to what you tell about. I wish you hadn't heard a word about it, and, another time, I wouldn't listen to petitions not intended for my ears."

The lawyer smiled.

"My dear fellow," he said, "you're wrong again. It was intended for my ears, and yours, too; and God Almighty intended it. My old mother used to sing about God's moving in a mysterious way, as I remember it."

"Well, my mother used to sing it, too," said the claimant, as he twisted the claim-papers in his fingers. "You can call in the morning, if you like, and tell 'mother' and 'him' the claim has been met."

"In a mysterious way," added the lawyer, smiling.

Neither this lesson nor the course of which it is a part is based upon an appeal to maudlin sentiment, but there can be no escape from the truth that *success,* in its highest and noblest form, brings one, finally, to view all human relationships with a feeling of deep emotion such as that which this lawyer felt when he overheard the old man's prayer.

It may be an old-fashioned idea, but somehow I can't get away from the belief that *no man can attain success in its highest form without the aid of earnest prayer!*

Prayer is the key with which one may open the secret doorway referred to in Lesson Eleven. In this age of mundane affairs, when the uppermost thought of the majority of people is centered upon the accumulation of wealth, or the struggle for a mere existence, it is both easy and natural for us to overlook the power of earnest prayer.

I am not saying that you should resort to prayer as a means of solving your daily problems which press for immediate attention; no, I am not going that far in a course of instruction which will be studied largely by those who are seeking in it the road to *success* that is measured in dollars; but, may I not modestly suggest to *you* that you, at least, give *prayer* a trial after *everything else fails* to bring you a *satisfying success?*

Thirty men, red-eyed and disheveled, lined up before the judge of the San Francisco police court. It was the regular morning company of drunks and disorderlies. Some were old and hardened; others hung their heads in shame. Just as the momentary disorder attending the bringing in of the prisoners quieted down, a strange thing happened. A strong, clear voice from below began singing:

> Last night I lay a-sleeping,
>> There came a dream so fair.

"Last night!" It had been for them all a nightmare or a drunken stupor. The song was such a contrast to the horrible fact that no one could fail of a sudden shock at the thought the song suggested.

> I stood in old Jerusalem,
>> Beside the Temple there,

the song went on. The judge had paused. He made a quiet inquiry. A former member of a famous opera company known all over the country was awaiting trial for forgery. It was he who was singing in his cell.

Meantime the song went on, and every man in the line showed emotion. One or two dropped on their knees; one boy at the end of the line, after a desperate effort at self-control, leaned against the wall, buried his face against his folded arms, and sobbed, "Oh, mother, mother."

The sobs, cutting to the very heart the men who heard, and the song, still welling its way through the court-room, blended in the hush. At length one man protested. "Judge," said he. "have we got to submit to this? We're here to take our punishment, but this—" He, too, began to sob.

It was impossible to proceed with the business of the court; yet the court gave no order to stop the song. The police sergeant, after an effort to keep the men in line, stepped back and waited with the rest. The song moved on to its climax:

Jerusalem, Jerusalem!
    Sing, for the night is o'er!
Hosanna, in the highest!
    Hosanna, for evermore!

In an ecstasy of melody the last words rang out, and then there was silence. The judge looked into the faces of the men before him. There was not one who was not touched by the song; not one in whom some better impulse was not stirred. He did not call the cases singly—a kind word of advice, and he dismissed them all. No man was fined or sentenced to the work-house that morning. The song had done more good than *punishment* could possibly have accomplished.

You have read the story of a Golden Rule lawyer and a Golden Rule judge. In these two commonplace incidents of every-day life you have observed how the Golden Rule works when *applied.*

A passive attitude toward the Golden Rule will bring no results; it is not enough merely to *believe* in the philosophy, while, at the same time, failing to *apply* it in your relationships with others. If you want results you must take an *active* attitude toward the Golden Rule. A mere passive attitude, represented by belief in its soundness, will avail you nothing.

Nor will it avail you anything to proclaim to the world your belief in the Golden Rule while your actions are not in harmony with your proclamation. Conversely stated, it will avail you nothing to appear to practice the Golden Rule, while, at heart, you are willing and eager to use this universal law of right conduct as a cloak to cover up a covetous and selfish nature. Murder will out. Even the most ignorant person will "sense" you for what you are.

"Human character does evermore publish itself. It will not be concealed. It hates darkness—it rushes into light…. I heard an experienced counselor say that he never feared the effect upon a jury of a lawyer who does not believe in his heart that his client ought to have a verdict. If he does not believe it, his unbelief will appear to the jury, despite all his protestations, and will become their unbelief. This is that law whereby a work of art, of whatever kind, sets us in the same state of mind wherein the artist was when he made it. That which we do not believe we cannot *adequately say,* though we may repeat the words ever so often. It was this conviction which Swedenborg expressed when he described a group of persons in the spiritual world endeavoring in vain to articulate a proposition which they did not believe; but they could not, though they twisted and folded their lips even to indignation.

> *A trifling kindness here*
>
> *and there,*
>
> *Is but a simple, small*
>
> *affair;*
>
> *Yet if your life has sown*
>
> *this free,*
>
> *Wide shall your*
>
> *happy harvest be.*

A man passes for what he is worth. What he is engraves itself on his face, on his form, on his fortunes, in letters of light which all men may read but himself.… If you would not be known to do anything, never do it. A man may play the fool in the drifts of a desert, but every grain of sand shall seem to see.

—EMERSON

It is the law upon which the Golden Rule philosophy is based to which Emerson has reference in the foregoing quotation. It was this same law that he had in mind when he wrote the following:

Every violation of truth is not only a sort of suicide in the liar, but is a stab at the health of human society. On the most profitable lie the course of events presently lays a destructive tax; whilst frankness proves to be the best tactics, for it invites frankness, puts the parties on a convenient footing and makes their business a friendship. Trust men and they will be true to you; treat them greatly and they will show themselves great, though they make an exception in your favor to all their rules of trade.

The Golden Rule philosophy is based upon a law which no man can circumvent. This law is the same law that is described in Lesson Eleven, on Accurate Thought, through the operation of which one's thoughts are transformed into reality corresponding exactly to the nature of the thoughts.

Once grant the creative power of our thought and there is an end of struggling for our own way, and an end of gaining it *at someone else's expense;* for, since by the terms of the hypothesis we can create what we like, the simplest way of getting what we want is, not to snatch it from somebody else, but to make it for ourselves; and, since there is no limit to thought there can be no need for straining, and for everyone to have his own way in *this manner*, would be to banish all strife, want, sickness, and sorrow from the earth.

Now, it is precisely on this assumption of the creative power of our thought that the whole Bible rests. If not, what is the meaning of being saved by Faith? Faith is essentially thought; and, therefore, every call to have faith in God is a call to trust in the power of our own thought about God. "According to your faith be it unto you," says the Old Testament. The entire book is nothing but one continuous statement of the creative power of Thought.

The Law of Man's Individuality is, therefore, the Law of Liberty, and equally it is the Gospel of peace; for when we truly understand the law of our own individuality, we see that the same law finds its expression in everyone else; and, consequently, we shall reverence *the law in others* exactly in proportion as we value it in ourselves. To do this is to follow the Golden Rule of doing to others what we would they should do unto us; and because we know that the Law of Liberty in ourselves must include the free use of our creative power, there is no longer any inducement to infringe the rights of others, for we can satisfy all our desires by the exercise of our knowledge of the law.

As this comes to be understood, co-operation will take the place of competition, with the result of removing all ground for enmity, whether between individuals, classes, or nations....

(The foregoing quotation is from *Bible Mystery and Bible Meaning* by the late Judge T. Troward, published by Robert McBride & Company, New York City. Judge Troward was the author of several interesting volumes, among them *The Edinburgh Lectures*, which is recommended to all students of this course.)

If you wish to know what happens to a man when he totally disregards the law upon which the Golden Rule philosophy is based, pick out any man in your community whom you know to live for the single dominating purpose of accumulating wealth, and who has no conscientious scruples as to how he accumulates that wealth. Study this man and you will observe that there is no warmth to his soul; there is no kindness to his words; there is no welcome to his face. He has become a slave to the desire for wealth; he is too busy to enjoy life and too selfish to wish to help others enjoy it. He walks, and talks, and breathes, but he is nothing but a human automaton. Yet there are many who envy such a man and wish that they might occupy his position, foolishly believing him to be a *success*.

There can never be *success* without happiness, and no man can be happy without dispensing happiness to others. Moreover, the dispensation must be voluntary and with no other object in view than that of spreading sunshine into the hearts of those whose hearts are heavy-laden with burdens.

George D. Herron had in mind the law upon which the Golden Rule philosophy is based when he said:

We have talked much of the brotherhood to come; but brotherhood has always been the fact of our life, long before it became a modern and inspired sentiment. Only we have been brothers in slavery and torment, brothers in ignorance and its perdition, brothers in disease, and war, and want, brothers in prostitution and hypocrisy. What happens to one of us sooner or later happens to all; we have always been unescapably involved in common destiny. The world constantly tends to the level of the downmost man in it; and that downmost man is the world's real ruler, hugging it close to his bosom, dragging it down to his death. You do not think so, but it is true, and it ought to be true. For if there were some way by which some of us could get free, apart from others, if there were some way by which some of us could have heaven while others had hell, if there were some way by which part of the world could escape some form of the blight and peril and misery of disinherited labor, then indeed would our world be lost and damned; but since men have never been able to separate themselves from one another's woes and wrongs, since history is fairly stricken with the lesson that we cannot escape brotherhood of some kind, since the whole of life is teaching us that we are hourly choosing between brotherhood in suffering and brotherhood in good, it remains for us to choose the brotherhood of a co-operative world, with all its fruits thereof—the fruits of *love* and *liberty*.

The world war ushered us into an age of cooperative effort in which the law of "live and let live" stands out like a shining star to guide us in our relationships with each other. This great universal call for co-operative effort is taking on many forms, not the I past important of which are the Rotary Clubs, the Kiwanis Clubs, the Lions Clubs and the many other luncheon clubs which bring men together in a spirit of friendly intercourse, for these clubs mark the beginning of an age of friendly competition in business. The next step will be a closer alliance of all such clubs in an out-and-out spirit of friendly co-operation.

The attempt by Woodrow Wilson and his contemporaries to establish the League of Nations, followed by the efforts of Warren G. Harding to give footing to the same cause under the name of the World Court, marked the first attempt in the history of the world to make the Golden Rule effective as a common meeting ground for the nations of the world.

There is no escape from the fact that the world has awakened to the truth in George D. Herron's statement that "we are hourly choosing between brotherhood in suffering and brotherhood in good." The world war has taught us—nay, forced upon us—the truth that a part of the world cannot suffer without injury to the whole world. These facts are called to your attention, not in the nature of a preachment on morality, but for the purpose of directing your attention to the underlying law through which these changes are being brought about.

For more than four thousand years the world has been thinking about the Golden Rule philosophy, and that *thought* is now becoming transformed into realization of the benefits that accrue to those who apply it.

Still mindful of the fact that the student of this course is interested in a material success that can be measured by bank balances, it seems appropriate to suggest here that all who will may profit by shaping their business philosophy to conform with this sweeping change toward co-operation which is taking place all over the world.

If you can grasp the significance of the tremendous change that has come over the world since the close of the world war, and if you can interpret the meaning of all the luncheon clubs and other similar gatherings which bring men and women together in a spirit of friendly co-operation, surely your imagination will suggest to you the fact that this is an opportune time to profit by adopting this spirit of friendly co-operation as the basis of your own business or professional philosophy.

> *No idle person is ever safe, whether he be rich or poor, white or black, educated or illiterate.*
>
> *—Booker T. Washington*

Stated conversely, it must be obvious to all who make any pretense of thinking accurately, that the time is at hand when failure to adopt the Golden Rule as the foundation of one's business or professional philosophy is the equivalent of economic suicide.

Perhaps you have wondered why the subject of *honesty* has not been mentioned in this course, as a prerequisite to *success,* and, if so, the answer will be found in this lesson. The Golden Rule philosophy, when rightly understood and applied, makes dishonesty impossible. It does more than this—it makes impossible all the other destructive qualities such as selfishness, greed, envy, bigotry, hatred and malice.

When you apply the Golden Rule, you become, at one and the same time, both the judge and the judged —the accused and the accuser. This places one in a position in which *honesty* begins in one's own heart, toward one's self, and extends to all others with equal effect. *Honesty* based upon the Golden Rule is not the brand of honesty which recognizes nothing but the question of expediency.

It is no credit to be honest, when honesty is obviously the most *profitable* policy, lest one lose a good customer or a valuable client or be sent to jail for trickery. But when honesty means either a temporary or a permanent material loss, then it becomes an *honor* of the highest degree to all who practice it. Such honesty has its appropriate reward in the accumulated power of character and reputation enjoyed by all who deserve it.

Those who understand and apply the Golden Rule philosophy are always scrupulously honest, not alone out of their desire to be just with others, but because of their desire to be just with themselves. They understand the eternal law upon which the Golden Rule is based, and they know that through the operation of this law *every thought they release and every act in which they indulge has its counterpart in some fact or circumstance with which they will later be confronted.*

Golden Rule philosophers are honest because they understand the truth that honesty adds to their own character that "vital something" which gives it life and power. Those who understand the law through which the Golden Rule operates would poison their own drinking water as quickly as they would indulge in acts of injustice to others, for they know that such injustice starts a chain of causation that will not only bring them physical suffering, but will destroy their characters, stain for ill their reputations and render impossible the attainment of enduring success.

The law through which the Golden Rule philosophy operates is none other than the law through which the principle of Autosuggestion operates. This statement gives you a suggestion from which you should be able to make a deduction of a far-reaching nature and of inestimable value.

Test your progress in the mastery of this course by analyzing the foregoing statement and determining, before you read on, what suggestion it offers you.

Of what possible benefit could it be to you to know that when you do unto others as if you were the others, which is the sum and substance of the Golden Rule, you are putting into motion a chain of causation through the aid of a law which affects the others according to the nature of your act, *and at the same time planting in your character, through your subconscious mind, the effects of that act?*

This question practically suggests its own answer, but as I am determined to cause you to think this vital subject out for yourself I will put the question in still another form, viz.:

If all your acts toward others, and even your thoughts of others, are registered in your sub-conscious mind, through the principle of Auto-suggestion, thereby building your own character in exact duplicate of your *thoughts* and *acts,* can you not see how important it is to guard those acts and thoughts?

We are now in the very heart of the real reason for doing unto others as we would have them do unto us, for it is obvious that whatever we do unto others we do unto ourselves.

Stated in another way, every *act* and every *thought* you release modifies your own character in exact conformity with the nature of the act or thought, and your character is a sort of center of magnetic attraction which attracts to you the people and conditions that harmonize with it.

You cannot indulge in an act toward another person without having first created the nature of that act in your own *thought, and you cannot release a thought without planting the sum and substance and nature of it in your own sub-conscious mind, there to become a part and parcel of your own character.*

Grasp this simple principle and you will understand why you cannot afford to hate or envy another person. You will also understand why you cannot afford to strike back, in kind, at those who do you an injustice. Likewise, you will understand the injunction, "Return good for evil."

Understand the law upon which the Golden Rule injunction is based and you will understand, also, the law that eternally binds all mankind in a single bond of fellowship and renders it impossible for you to injure another person, by *thought* or *deed,* without injuring yourself; and, likewise, adds to your own character the results of every kind *thought* and *deed* in which you indulge.

Understand this law and you will then know, beyond room for the slightest doubt, that you are constantly punishing yourself for every wrong you commit and rewarding yourself for every act of constructive conduct in which you indulge.

It seems almost an act of Providence that the greatest wrong and the most severe injustice ever done me by one of my fellow men was done just as I began this lesson. (Some of the students of this course will know what it is to which I refer.)

This injustice has worked a temporary hardship on me, but that is of little consequence compared to the advantage it has given me by providing a timely opportunity for me to test the soundness of the entire premise upon which this lesson is founded.

The injustice to which I refer left two courses of action open to me. I could have claimed relief by "striking back" at my antagonist, through both civil court action and criminal libel proceedings, or I could have stood upon my right to forgive him. One course of action would have brought me a substantial sum of money and whatever joy and satisfaction there may be in defeating and *punishing* an enemy. The other course of action would have brought me self-respect which is enjoyed by those who have successfully met the test and discovered that they have evolved to the point at which they can repeat the Lord's Prayer and *mean it!*

I chose the latter course. I did so, despite the recommendations of close personal friends to "strike back," and despite the offer of a prominent lawyer to do my "striking" for me *without cost.*

But the lawyer offered to do the impossible, for the reason that no man can "strike back" at another *without cost.* Not always is the cost of a monetary nature, for there are other things with which one may pay that are dearer than money.

It would be as hopeless to try to make one who was not familiar with the law upon which the Golden Rule is based understand why I refused to strike back at this enemy as it would to try to describe the law of gravitation to an ape. If you understand this law you understand, also, why I chose to *forgive* my enemy.

In the Lord's Prayer we are admonished to forgive our enemies, but that admonition will fall on deaf ears except where the listener understands the law upon which it is based. That law is none other than the law upon which the Golden Rule is based. It is the law that forms the foundation of this entire lesson, and through which we must inevitably reap that which we sow. There is no escape from the operation of this law, nor is there any cause to try to avoid its consequences if we refrain from putting into motion *thoughts* and *acts* that are destructive.

That we may more concretely describe the law upon which this lesson is based, let us embody the law in a code of ethics such as one who wishes to follow literally the injunction of the Golden Rule might appropriately adopt, as follows.

> *There is no defeat except from within. There is really no insurmountable barrier save your own inherent weakness of purpose.*
>
> *–Emerson*

MY CODE OF ETHICS

1. I believe in the Golden Rule as the basis of all human conduct; therefore, I will never do to another person that which I would not be willing for that person to do to me if our positions were reversed.

II. I will be honest, even to the slightest detail, in all my transactions with others, not alone because of my desire to be fair with them, but because of my desire to impress the idea of honesty on my own subconscious mind, thereby weaving this essential quality into my own character.

III. I will forgive those who are unjust toward me, with no thought as to whether they deserve it or not because I understand the law through which forgiveness of others strengthens my own character and wipes out the effects of my own transgressions, in my sub-conscious mind.

IV. I will be just, generous and fair with others always even though I know that these acts will go unnoticed and unrewarded, in the ordinary terms of reward, because I understand and intend to apply the law through the aid of which one's own character is but the sum total of one's own *acts* and *deeds*.

V. Whatever time I may have to devote to the discovery and exposure of the weaknesses and faults of others I will devote, more profitably, to the discovery and *correction* of my own.

VI. I will slander no person, no matter how much I may believe another person may deserve it, because I wish to plant no destructive suggestions in my own sub-conscious mind.

VII. I recognize the power of Thought as being an inlet leading into my brain from the universal ocean of life; therefore, I will set no destructive thoughts afloat upon that ocean lest they pollute the minds of others.

VIII. I will conquer the common human tendency toward hatred, and envy; and selfishness, and jealousy, and malice, and pessimism, and doubt, and fear; for I believe these to be the seed from which the world harvests most of its troubles.

IX. When my mind is not occupied with thoughts that tend toward the attainment of my *definite chief aim* in life, I will voluntarily keep it filled with thoughts of courage, and self-confidence, and good-will toward others, and faith, and kindness, and loyalty, and love for truth, and justice, for I believe these to be the seed from which the world reaps its harvest of progressive growth.

x. I understand that a mere passive belief in the soundness of the Golden Rule philosophy is of no value whatsoever, either to myself or to others; therefore, I will *actively* put into operation this universal rule for good in all my transactions with others.

xi. I understand the law through the operation of which my own character is developed from my own *acts* and *thoughts;* therefore, I will guard with care all that goes into its development.

xii. Realizing that enduring happiness comes only through helping others find it; that no act of kindness is without its reward, even though it may never be directly repaid, I will do my best to assist others when and where the opportunity appears.

You have noticed frequent reference to Emerson throughout this course. Every student of the course should own a copy of Emerson's *Essays,* and the essay on Compensation should be read and studied at least every three months. Observe, as you read this essay, that it deals with the same law as that upon which the Golden Rule is based.

There are people who believe that the Golden Rule philosophy is nothing more than a theory, and that it is in no way connected with an immutable law. They have arrived at this conclusion because of personal experience wherein they rendered service to others without enjoying the benefits of direct reciprocation.

How many are there who have not rendered service to others that was neither reciprocated nor appreciated? I am sure that I have had such an experience, not once, but many times, and I am equally sure that I will have similar experiences in the future, nor will I discontinue rendering service to others merely because *they* neither reciprocate nor appreciate my efforts.

And here is the reason:

When I render service to another, or indulge in an act of kindness, I store away in my sub-conscious mind the effect of my efforts, which may be likened to the "charging" of an electric battery. By and by, if I indulge in a sufficient number of such acts I will have developed a positive, dynamic character that will *attract* to me people who harmonize with or resemble my own character.

Those whom I *attract* to me will reciprocate the acts of kindness and the service that I have rendered others, thus the Law of Compensation will have balanced the scales of justice for me, bringing back from one source the results of service that I rendered through an entirely different source.

> *You have not fulfilled every duty unless you have fulfilled that of being pleasant.*
>
> *– Charles Buxton*

You have often heard it said that a salesman's first sale should be to himself, which means that unless he first convinces himself of the merits of his wares he will not be able to convince others. Here, again, enters this same Law of Attraction, for it is a well known fact that *enthusiasm* is contagious, and when a salesman shows great *enthusiasm* over his wares he will arouse a corresponding interest in the minds of others.

You can comprehend this law quite easily by regarding yourself as a sort of human magnet that attracts those whose characters harmonize with your own. In thus regarding yourself as a magnet that attracts to you all who harmonize with your dominating characteristics and repels all who do not so harmonize, you should keep in mind, also, the fact that *you are the builder of that magnet;* also, that you may change its nature so that it will correspond to any ideal that you may wish to set up and follow.

And, most important of all, you should keep in mind the fact that this entire process of change takes place through *thought!*

Your character is but the sum total of your *thoughts* and *deeds!* This truth has been stated in many different ways throughout this course.

Because of this great truth it is impossible for you to render any useful service or indulge in any act of kindness toward others without benefiting thereby. Moreover, it is just as impossible for you to indulge in any destructive *act* or *thought* without paying the penalty in the loss of a corresponding amount of your own power.

Positive thought develops a dynamic personality. *Negative thought* develops a personality of an opposite nature. In many of the preceding lessons of this course, and in this one, definite instructions are given as to the exact method of developing personality through *positive thought*. These instructions are particularly detailed in Lesson Three, on *Self-confidence*. In that lesson you have a very definite formula to follow. All of the formulas provided in this course are for the purpose of helping you *consciously* to direct the power of *thought* in the development of a personality that will attract to you those who will be of help in the attainment of your *definite chief aim*.

You need no proof that your hostile or unkind *acts* toward others bring back the effects of retaliation. Moreover, this retaliation is usually definite and immediate. Likewise, you need no proof that you can accomplish more by dealing with others in such a way that they will want to co-operate with you. If you mastered the eighth lesson, on Self-control, you now understand how to induce others to act toward you as you wish them to act—*through your own attitude toward them*.

The law of "an eye for an eye and a tooth for a tooth" is based upon the selfsame law as that upon which the Golden Rule operates. This is nothing more than the law of retaliation with which all of us are familiar. Even the most selfish person will respond to this law, *because he cannot help it!* If I speak ill of you, even though I tell the truth, you will not think kindly of me. Furthermore, you will most likely retaliate in kind. But, if I speak of your virtues you will think kindly of me, and when the opportunity appears you will reciprocate in kind in the majority of instances.

Through the operation of this law of attraction the uninformed are constantly attracting trouble and grief and hatred and opposition from others by their *unguarded words* and *destructive acts.*

Do unto others as you would have them do unto you!

We have heard that injunction expressed thousands of times, yet how many of us understand the law upon which it is based? To make this injunction somewhat clearer it might be well to state it more in detail, about as follows:

Do unto others as you would have them do unto you, *bearing in mind the fact that human nature has a tendency to retaliate in kind.*

Confucius must have had in mind the law of retaliation when he stated the Golden Rule philosophy in about this way:

Do not unto others that which you would not have them do unto you.

And he might well have added an explanation to the effect that the reason for his injunction was based upon the common tendency of man to retaliate in kind.

Those who do not understand the law upon which the Golden Rule is based are inclined to argue that it will not work, for the reason that men are inclined toward the principle of exacting "an eye for an eye and a tooth for a tooth," which is nothing more nor less than the law of retaliation. If they would go a step further in their reasoning they would understand that they are looking at the *negative* effects of this law, and that the selfsame law is capable of producing *positive* effects as well.

In other words, if you would not have your own eye plucked out, then insure against this misfortune by refraining from plucking out the other fellow's eye. Go a step further and render the other fellow an act of kindly, helpful service, and *through the operation of this same law of retaliation* he will render you a similar service.

And, if he should fail to reciprocate your kindness —what then?

You have profited, nevertheless, because of the effect of your act on *your own sub-conscious mind!*

Thus by indulging in acts of kindness and applying, always, the Golden Rule philosophy, you are sure of benefit from one source and at the same time you have a pretty fair chance of profiting from another source.

It might happen that you would base all of your acts toward others on the Golden Rule without enjoying any direct reciprocation for a long period of time, and it might so happen that those to whom you rendered those acts of kindness would never reciprocate, but meantime you have been adding vitality to your own character and sooner or later this *positive character* which you have been building will begin to assert itself and you will discover that you have been receiving compound interest on compound interest in return for those acts of kindness which appeared to have been wasted on those who neither appreciated nor reciprocated them.

Remember that your *reputation* is made by others, but your *character* is made by *you!*

You want your reputation to be a favorable one, but you cannot be sure that it will be for the reason that it is something that exists outside of your own control, in the minds of others. It is what others believe you to be. With your character it is different. Your character is that which *you are,* as the results of your *thoughts* and *deeds*. You control it. You can make it weak, good or bad. When you are satisfied and know in your mind that your character is above reproach you need not worry about your reputation, for it is as impossible for your character to be destroyed or damaged by anyone except yourself as it is to destroy matter or energy.

It was this truth that Emerson had in mind when he said: "A political victory, a rise of rents, the recovery of your sick or the return of your absent friend, or some other quite external event raises your spirits and you think your days are prepared for you. *Do not believe it.* It can never be so. *Nothing can bring you peace but yourself. Nothing can bring you peace but the triumph of principles.*"

One reason for being just toward others is the fact that such action may cause them to reciprocate, in kind, but a better reason is the fact that kindness and justice toward others develop *positive character* in all who indulge in these acts.

You may withhold from me the reward to which I am entitled for rendering you helpful service, but ne one can deprive me of the benefit I will derive from the rendering of that service in so far as it adds to my own *character*.

We are living in a great industrial age. Everywhere we see the evolutionary forces working great changes in the method and manner of living, and rearranging the relationships between men, in the ordinary pursuit of life, liberty and a living.

This is an age of organized effort. On every hand we see evidence that organization is the basis of all financial success, and while other factors than that of organization enter into the attainment of success, this factor is still one of major importance.

This industrial age has created two comparatively new terms. One is called "capital" and the other "labor." Capital and labor constitute the main wheels in the machinery of organized effort. These two great forces enjoy success in exact ratio to the extent that both understand and apply the Golden Rule philosophy. Despite this fact, however, harmony between these two forces does not always prevail, thanks to the destroyers of confidence who make a living by sowing the seed of dissension and stirring up strife between employers and employees.

During the past fifteen years I have devoted considerable time to the study of the causes of disagreement between employers and employees. Also, I have gathered much information on this subject from other men who, likewise, have been studying this problem.

There is but one solution which will, if understood by all concerned, bring harmony out of chaos and establish a perfect working relationship between capital and labor. The remedy is no invention of mine. It is based upon a great universal law of Nature. This remedy has been well stated by one of the great men of this generation, in the following words:

> The question we propose to consider is exciting deep interest at the present time, but no more than its importance demands. It is one of the hopeful signs of the times that these subjects of vital interest to human happiness are constantly coming up for a hearing, are engaging the attention of the wisest men, and stirring the minds of all classes of people. The wide prevalence of this movement shows that a new life is beating in the heart of humanity, operating upon their faculties like the warm breath of spring upon the frozen ground and the dormant germs of the plant. It will make a great stir, it will break up many frozen and dead forms, it will produce great and, in some cases, it may be, destructive changes, but it announces the blossoming of new hopes, and the coming of new harvests for the supply of human wants and the means of greater happiness. There is great need of wisdom to guide the new forces coming into action. Every man is under the most solemn obligation to do his part in forming a correct public opinion and giving wise direction to popular will.

> The only solution for the problems of labor, of want, of abundance, of suffering and sorrow can only be found by regarding them from a moral and spiritual point of view. They must be seen and examined in a light that is not of themselves. *The true relations of labor and capital can never be discovered by human selfishness.* They must be viewed from a higher purpose than wages or the accumulation of wealth. They must be regarded from their bearing upon the purposes for which man was created. It is from this point of view I propose to consider the subject before us.

Capital and labor are essential to each other. Their interests are so bound together that they cannot be separated. In civilized and enlightened communities they are mutually dependent. If there is any difference, capital is more dependent upon labor than labor upon capital. Life can be sustained without capital. Animals, with a few exceptions, have no property, and take no anxious thought for the morrow, and our Lord commends them to our notice as examples worthy of imitation. "Behold the fowls of the air," He says, "for they sow not, neither do they reap nor gather into barns, yet your heavenly Father feedeth them." The savages live without capital. Indeed, the great mass of human beings live by their labor from day to day, from hand to mouth. But no man can live upon his wealth. He cannot eat his gold and silver; he cannot clothe himself with deeds and certificates of stock. Capital can do nothing without labor, *and its only value consists in its power to purchase labor or its results.* It is itself the product of labor. It has no occasion, therefore, to assume an importance that does not belong to it. Absolutely dependent, however, as it is upon labor for its value, it is an essential factor in human progress.

The moment man begins to rise from a savage and comparatively independent state to a civilized and dependent one, capital becomes necessary. Men come into more intimate relations with one another. Instead of each one doing everything, men begin to devote themselves to special employments, and to depend upon others to provide many things for them while they engage in some special occupation. In this way labor becomes diversified. One man works in iron, another in wood; one manufactures cloth, another makes it into garments; some raise food to feed those who build houses and manufacture implements of husbandry. This necessitates a system of exchanges, and to facilitate exchanges roads must be made, and men must be employed to make them. As population increases and necessities multiply, the business of exchange becomes enlarged, until we have immense manufactories, railroads girding the earth with iron bands, steamships plowing every sea, and a multitude of men who cannot raise bread or make a garment, or do anything directly for the supply of their own wants.

Now, we can see how we become more dependent upon others as our wants are multiplied and civilization advances. Each one works in his special employment, does better work, because he can devote his whole thought and time to a form of use for which he is specially fitted, and contributes more largely to the public good. While he is working for others, all others are working for him. Every member of the community is working for the whole body, and the whole body for every member. This is the law of perfect life, a law which rules everywhere in the material body. Every man who is engaged in any employment useful to body or mind is a philanthropist, a public benefactor, whether he raises corn on the prairie, cotton in Texas or India, mines coal in the chambers of the earth, or feeds it to engines in the hold of a steamship. If selfishness did not pervert and blast human motives, all men and women would be fulfilling the law of charity while engaged in their daily employment.

To carry on this vast system of exchanges, to place the forest and the farm, the factory and the mine side by side, and deliver the products of all climes at every door, requires immense capital. One man cannot work his farm or factory, and build a railroad or a line of steamships. As raindrops acting singly cannot drive a mill or supply steam for an engine, but, collected in a vast reservoir, become the resistless power of Niagara, or the force which drives the engine and steamship like mighty shuttles from mountain to seacoast and from shore to shore, so a few dollars in a multitude of pockets are powerless to provide the means for these vast operations, but combined they move the world.

Capital is a friend of labor and essential to its economical exercise and just reward. It can be, and often is, a terrible enemy, when employed for selfish purposes alone; but the great mass of it is more friendly to human happiness than is generally supposed. It cannot be employed without in some way, either directly or indirectly, helping the laborer. We think of the evils we suffer, but allow the good we enjoy to pass unnoticed. We think of the evils that larger means would relieve and the comforts they would provide, but overlook the blessings we enjoy that would have been impossible without large accumulations of capital. It is the part of wisdom to form a just estimate of the good we receive as well as the evils we suffer.

It is a common saying at the present time, that the rich are growing richer and the poor poorer; but when all man's possessions are taken into the account there are good reasons for doubting this assertion. It is true that the rich are growing richer. It is also true that the condition of the laborer is constantly improving. *The common laborer has conveniences and comforts which princes could not command a century ago.* He is better clothed, has a greater variety and abundance of food, lives in a more comfortable dwelling, and has many more conveniences for the conduct of domestic affairs and the prosecution of labor than money could purchase but a few years ago. An emperor could not travel with the ease, the comfort, and the swiftness that the common laborer can today. He may think that he stands alone, with no one to help. But, in truth, he has an immense retinue of servants constantly waiting upon him, ready and anxious to do his bidding. It requires a vast army of men and an immense outlay of capital to provide a common dinner, such as every man and woman, with few exceptions, has enjoyed today.

Think of the vast combination of means and men and forces necessary to provide even a frugal meal. The Chinaman raises your tea, the Brazilian your coffee, the East Indian your spices, the Cuban your sugar, the farmer upon the western prairies your bread and possibly your beef, the gardener your vegetables, the dairyman your butter and milk; the miner has dug from the hills the coal with which your food was cooked and your house was warmed, the cabinet-maker has provided you with chairs and tables, the cutler with knives and forks, the potter with dishes, the Irishman has made your table-cloth, the butcher has dressed your meat, the miller your flour.

But these various articles of food, and the means of preparing and serving them, were produced at immense distances from you and from one another. Oceans had to be traversed, hills leveled, valleys filled, and mountains tunneled, ships must be built, railways constructed, and a vast army of men instructed and employed in every mechanical art before the materials for your dinner could be prepared and served. There must also be men to collect these materials, to buy and sell and distribute them. Everyone stands in his own place and does his own work, and receives his wages. But he is none the less working for you, and serving you as truly and effectively as he would be if he were in your special employment and received his wages from your hand. In the light of these facts, which everyone must acknowledge, we may be able to see more clearly the truth, that every man and woman who does useful work is a public benefactor, and the thought of it and the purpose of it will ennoble the labor and the laborer.

We are all bound together by common ties. The rich and the poor, the learned and the ignorant, the strong and the weak, are woven together in one social and civic web. Harm to one is harm to all; help to one is help to all.

You see what a vast army of servants it requires to provide your dinner. Do you not see that it demands a corresponding amount of capital to provide and keep this complicated machinery in motion? And do you not see that every man, woman and child is enjoying the benefit of it? How could we get our coal, our meat, our flour, our tea and coffee, sugar and rice? The laborer cannot build ships and sail them and support himself while doing it. *The farmer cannot leave his farm and take his produce to the market. The miner cannot mine and transport his coal.* The farmer in Kansas may be burning corn today to cook his food and warm his dwelling, and the miner may be hungry for the bread which the corn would supply, because they cannot exchange the fruits of their labor. Every acre of land, every forest and mine has been increased in value by railways and steamboats, and the comforts of life and the means of social and intellectual culture have been carried to the most inaccessible places.

But the benefits of capital are not limited to supplying present wants and comforts. It opens new avenues for labor. It diversifies it and gives a wider field to everyone to do the kind of work for which he is best fitted by natural taste and genius. The number of employments created by railways, steamships, telegraph, and manufactories by machinery can hardly be estimated. Capital is also largely invested in supplying the means of intellectual and spiritual culture.

Books are multiplied at constantly diminishing prices, and the best thought of the world, by means of our great publishing houses, is made accessible to the humblest workman. There is no better example of the benefits the common laborer derives from capital than the daily newspaper. For two or three cents the history of the world for twenty-four hours is brought to every door. The laborer, while riding to or from his work in a comfortable car, can visit all parts of the known world and get a truer idea of the events of the day than he could if he were bodily present. A battle in China or Africa, an earthquake in Spain, a dynamite explosion in London, a debate in Congress, the movements of men in public and private life for the suppression of vice, for enlightening the ignorant, helping the needy, and improving the people generally; are spread before him in a small compass, and bring him into contact and on equality, in regard to the world's history, with kings and queens, with saints and sages, and people in every condition in life. *Do you ever think,* while reading the morning paper, how many men have been running on your errands, collecting intelligence for you from all parts of the earth, and putting it into a form convenient for your use? It required the investment of millions of money and the employment of thousands of men to produce that paper and leave it at your door. And what did all this service cost you? A few cents.

These are examples of the benefits which everyone derives from capital, benefits which could not be obtained without vast expenditures of money; benefits which come to us without our care and lay their blessings at our feet. Capital cannot be invested in any useful production without blessing a multitude of people. It sets the machinery of life in motion, it multiplies employment; it places the product of all climes at every door, it draws the people of all nations together; brings mind in contact with mind, and gives to every man and woman a large and valuable share of the product.

These are facts which it would be well for everyone, however poor he may be, to consider.

If capital is such a blessing to labor; if it can only be brought into use by labor, and derives all its value from it, how can there be any conflict between them? There could be none if both the capitalist and laborer acted from humane and Christian principles. But they do not. They are governed by inhuman and unchristian principles. Each party seeks to get the largest returns for the least service. Capital desires larger profits, labor higher wages. The interests of the capitalist and the laborer come into direct collision. In this warfare capital has great advantages, and has been prompt to take them. It has demanded and taken the lion's share of the profits. It has despised the servant that enriched it. It has regarded the laborer as a menial, a slave, whose rights and happiness it was not bound to respect. It influences legislators to enact laws in its favor, subsidizes governments and wields its power for its own advantage. Capital has been a lord and labor a servant. While the servant remained docile and obedient, content with such compensation as its lord chose to give, there was no conflict. But labor is rising from a servile, submissive, and hopeless condition. It has acquired strength and intelligence; has gained the idea that it has rights that ought to be respected, and begins to assert and combine to support them.

Each party in this warfare regards the subject from its own selfish interests. The capitalist supposes that gain to labor is loss to him, and that he must look to his own interests first; that the cheaper the labor the larger his gains. Consequently it is for his interest to keep the price as low as possible. On the contrary, the laborer thinks that he loses what the capitalist gains, and, consequently, that it is for his interest to get as large wages as possible. From these opposite points of view their interests appear to be directly hostile. What one party gains the other loses; hence the conflict. Both are acting from selfish motives, and, consequently, must be wrong. Both parties see only half of the truth, and, mistaking that for the whole of it, they fall into a mistake ruinous to both. Each one stands on his own ground, and regards the subject wholly from his point of view and in the misleading light of his own selfishness. Passion inflames the mind and blinds the understanding; and when passion is aroused men will sacrifice their own interests to injure others, and both will suffer loss. They will wage continual warfare against each other; they will resort to all devices, and take advantage of every necessity to win a victory. Capital tries to starve the laborer into submission, like a beleaguered city; and hunger and want are most powerful weapons. Labor sullenly resists, and tries to destroy the value of capital by rendering it unproductive. If necessity or interest compels a truce, it is a sullen one, and maintained with the purpose of renewing hostilities as soon as there is any prospect of success. Thus laborers and capitalists confront each other like two armed hosts, ready at any time to renew the conflict. *It will be renewed, without doubt, and continued with varying success until both parties discover that they are mistaken, that their interests are mutual, and can only be secured to the fullest extent by co-operation and giving to each the reward it deserves.* The capitalist and the laborer must clasp hands across the bottomless pit into which so much wealth and work has been cast.

How this reconciliation is to be effected is a question that is occupying the minds of many wise and good men on both sides at the present time. Wise and impartial legislation will, no doubt, be an important agent in restraining blind passion and protecting all classes from insatiable greed; and it is the duty of every man to use his best endeavors to secure such legislation both in state and national governments. Organizations of laborers for protecting their own rights and securing a better reward for their labor, will have a great influence. That influence will continue to increase as their temper becomes normal and firm, and their demands are based *on justice and humanity.* Violence and threats will effect no good. Dynamite, whether in the form of explosives or the more destructive force of fierce and reckless passion, will heal no wounds nor subdue any hostile feeling. Arbitration is, doubtless, the wisest and most practicable means now available to bring about amicable relations between these hostile parties and secure justice to both. Giving the laborer a share in the profits of the business has worked well in some cases, but it is attended with great practical difficulties which require more wisdom, self-control and genuine regard for the common interests of both parties than often can be found. Many devices may have a partial and temporary effect. But no permanent progress can be made in settling this conflict without restraining and finally removing its cause.

Its real central cause is an inordinate love of self and the world, and that cause will continue to operate as long as it exists. It may be restrained and moderated, but it will assert itself when occasion offers. Every wise man must, therefore, seek to remove the cause, and as far as he can do it he will control effects. Purify the fountain, and you make the whole stream pure and wholesome.

There is a principle of universal influence that must underlie and guide every successful effort to bring these two great factors of human good which now confront each other with hostile purpose, into harmony. It is no invention or discovery of mine. It embodies a higher than human wisdom. It is not difficult to understand or apply. The child can comprehend it and act according to it. It is universal in its application, and wholly useful in its effects. It will lighten the burdens of labor and increase its rewards. It will give security to capital and make it more productive. It is simply the Golden Rule, embodied in these words: *"Therefore all things whatsoever ye would that men should do to you, do ye even so to them: for this is the law and the prophets."*

Before proceeding to apply this principle to the case in hand, let me call your special attention to it. It is a very remarkable law of human life which seems to have been generally over-looked by statesmen, philosophers and religious teachers. This rule embodies the whole of religion; it comprises all the pre-cepts, commandments, and means of the future triumphs of good over evil, of truth over error, and the peace and happiness of men, foretold in the glorious visions of the prophets. Mark the words. It does not merely say that it is a wise rule; that it accords with the principles of the Divine order revealed in the law and the prophets. *It embodies them all; it "is the law and the prophets."* It comprises love to God. It says we should regard Him as we desire to have Him regard us; that we should do to Him as we wish to have Him do to us. If we desire to have Him love us with all His heart, with all His soul, with all His mind, and with all His strength, we must love Him in the same manner. If we desire to have our neighbor love us as he loves himself, we must love him as we love ourself. Here, then, is the universal and Divine law of human service and fellow-ship. It is not a precept of human wisdom; it has its origin in the Divine nature, and its embodiment in human nature. Now, let us apply it to the conflict between labor and capital.

You are a capitalist. Your money is invested in manufac-tures, in land, in mines, in merchandise, railways, and ships, or you loan it to others on interest. You employ, directly or indirectly, men to use your capital. You cannot come to a just conclusion concerning your rights and duties and privileges by looking wholly at your own gains. The glitter of the silver and gold will exercise so potent a spell over your mind that it will blind you to everything else. You can see no interest but your own. The laborer is not known or regarded as a man who has any interests you are bound to regard. You see him only as your slave, your tool, your means of adding to your wealth. In this light he is a friend so far as he serves you, an enemy so far as he does not. But change your point of view. Put yourself in his place; put him in your place. How would you like to have him treat you if you were in his place? Perhaps you have been there. In all probability you have, for the capitalist today was the laborer yesterday, and the laborer today will be the employer tomorrow. You know from lively and painful experience how you would like to be treated. Would you like to be regarded as a mere tool? As a means of enriching another? Would you like to have your wages kept down to the bare necessities of life? Would you like to be regarded with indifference and treated with brutality? Would you like to have your blood, your strength, your soul coined into dollars for the benefit of another? These questions are easy to answer. Everyone knows that he would rejoice to be treated kindly, to have his interests regarded, his rights recognized and protected. Everyone knows that such regard awakens a response in his own heart. Kindness begets kindness; respect awakens respect. Put yourself in his place. Imagine that you are dealing with yourself, and you will have no difficulty in deciding whether you should give the screw another turn, that you may wring a penny more from the muscles of the worker, or relax its pressure, and, if possible, add something to his wages, and give him respect for his service. Do to him as you would have him do to you in changed conditions.

You are a laborer. You receive a certain sum for a day's work. Put yourself in the place of your employer. How would you like to have the men you employed work for you? Would you think it right that they should regard you as their enemy? Would you think it honest in them to slight their work, *to do as little and to get as much as possible?* If you had a large contract which must be completed at a fixed time or you would suffer great loss, would you like to have your work-men take advantage of your necessity to compel an increase of their wages? Would you think it right and wise in them to interfere with you in the management of your business? To dictate whom you should employ, and on what terms you should employ them? Would you not rather have them do honest work in a kind and good spirit? Would you not be much more disposed to look to their interests, to lighten their labor, to increase their wages when you could afford to do so, and look after the welfare of their families, when you found that they regarded yours? I know that it would be so. It is true that men are selfish, and that some men are so mean and contracted in spirit that they cannot see any interest but their own; whose hearts, not made of flesh but of silver and gold, are so hard that they are not touched by any human feeling, and care not how much others suffer if they can make a cent by it. But they are the exception, not the rule. We are influenced by the regard and devotion of others to our interests. The laborer who knows that his employer feels kindly toward him, desires to treat him justly and to regard his good, will do better work and more of it, and will be disposed to look to his employer's interests as well as his own.

I am well aware that many will think this Divine and humane law of doing to others as we would have them do to us, is impracticable in this selfish and worldly age. If both parties

would be governed by it, everyone can see how happy would
be the results. But, it will be said, they will not. The laborer
will not work unless compelled by want. He will take advantage of every necessity. As soon as he gains a little independence of his employer he becomes proud, arrogant and
hostile. The employer will seize upon every means to keep
the workmen dependent upon him, and to make as much
out of them as possible. Every inch of ground which labor
yields capital will occupy and intrench itself in it, and from
its vantage bring the laborer into greater dependence and
more abject submission. But this is a mistake. The history of
the world testifies that when the minds of men are not em-
bittered by intense hostility and their feelings outraged by
cruel wrongs, they are ready to listen to calm, disinterested
and judicious counsel. A man who employed a large number
of laborers in mining coal told me that he had never known
an instance to fail of a calm and candid response when he
had appealed to honorable motives, as a man to man, both
of whom acknowledged a common humanity. There is a
recent and most notable instance in this city of the happy
effect of calm, disinterested and judicious counsel in settling difficulties between employers and workmen that were
disastrous to both.

When the mind is inflamed by passion men will not listen
to reason. They become blind to their own interests and regardless of the interests of others. *Difficulties are never settled
while passion rages. They are never settled by conflict. One party
may be subdued by power; but the sense of wrong will remain;
the fire of passion will slumber ready to break out again on the
first occasion.* But let the laborer or the capitalist feel assured
that the other party has no wish to take any advantage, that
there is a sincere desire and determination on both sides to
be just and pay due regard to their common interests, and

all the conflict between them would cease, as the wild waves of the ocean sink to calm when the winds are at rest. The laborer and the capitalist have a mutual and common interest. Neither can permanently prosper without the prosperity of the other. They are parts of one body. If labor is the arm, capital is the blood. Devitalize or waste the blood, and the arm loses its power. Destroy the arm, and the blood is useless. Let each care for the other, and both are benefited. *Let each take the Golden Rule as a guide,* and all cause of hostility will be removed, all conflict will cease, and they will go hand in hand to do their work and reap their just reward.

If you have mastered the fundamentals upon which this lesson is based, you understand why it is that no public speaker can move his audience or convince men of his argument unless he, himself, believes that which he is saying.

You also understand why no salesman can convince his prospective purchaser unless he has first convinced himself of the merits of his goods.

Throughout this entire course one particular principle has been emphasized for the purpose of illustrating the truth that every personality is the sum total of the individual's *thoughts* and *acts* — that we come to resemble the nature of our dominating *thoughts*.

Thought is the only power that can systematically organize, accumulate and assemble facts and materials according to a definite plan. A flowing river can assemble dirt and build land, and a storm can gather and assemble sticks into a shapeless mass of debris, but neither storms nor river can *think;* therefore, the materials which they assemble are not assembled in organized, definite form.

Man, alone, has the power to transform his *thoughts* into physical reality; man, alone, can dream and make his dreams come true.

Man has the power to create ideals and rise to their attainment.

How did it happen that man is the only creature on earth that knows how to use the power of *thought?* It "happened" because man is the apex of the pyramid of evolution, the product of millions of years of struggle during which man has risen above the other creatures of the earth *as the result of his own thoughts and their effects upon himself.*

Just when, where and how the first rays of *thought* began to flow into man's brain no one knows, but we all know that thought is the power which distinguishes man from all other creatures; likewise, we all know that *thought* is the power that has enabled man to lift himself above all other creatures.

No one knows the limitations of the power of *thought,* or whether or not it has any limitations. Whatever man *believes* he can do he eventually does. But a few generations back the more imaginative writers dared to write of travel in space, and lo! it became a reality and is now a common event. Through the evolutionary power of *thought* the hopes and ambitions of one generation become a reality in the next.

The power of *thought* has been given the dominating position throughout this course, for the reason that it belongs in that position. Man's dominating position in the world is the direct result of *thought,* and it must be this power that you, as an individual, will use in the attainment of *success,* no matter what may be your idea of what represents *success.*

You have now arrived at the point at which you should take inventory of yourself for the purpose of ascertaining what qualities you need to give you a well balanced and rounded out personality.

Fifteen major factors entered into the building of this course. Analyze yourself carefully, with the assistance of one or more other persons if you feel that you need it, for the purpose of ascertaining in which of the fifteen factors of this course you are the weakest, and then concentrate your efforts upon those particular lessons until you have fully developed those factors which they represent.

INDECISION

AN AFTER-THE-LESSON VISIT WITH THE AUTHOR

Time!

Procrastination robs you of opportunity. It is a significant fact that no great leader was ever known to procrastinate. You are fortunate if AMBITION drives you into action, never permitting you to falter or turn back, once you have rendered a DECISION to go forward. Second by second, as the clock ticks off the distance TIME is running a race with YOU. Delay means defeat, because no man may ever make up a second of lost TIME. TIME is a master worker which heals the wounds of failure and disappointment and rights all wrongs and turns all mistakes into capital, but, it favors only those who kill off procrastination and remain in ACTION when decisions are to made.

Life is a great checker-board. The player opposite you is TIME.

If you hesitate you will be wiped off the board. If you keep moving you may win. The only real capital is TIME, but it is capital only when used.

You may be shocked if you keep accurate account of the TIME you waste in a single day. Take a look at the picture above if you wish to know the fate of all who play carelessly with TIME.

THE PICTURE AT top of the previous page tells a true story of one of the chief causes of FAILURE! One of the players is "TIME" and the other is Mr. Average Man; let us call him YOU.

Move by move Time has wiped off Mr. Average Man's men until he is finally cornered, where Time will get him, no matter which way he moves. INDECISION has driven him into the corner.

Ask any well informed salesman and he will tell you that indecision is the outstanding weakness of the majority of people. Every salesman is familiar with that time-worn alibi, "I will think it over," which is the last trench-line of defense of those who have not the courage to say either yes or no. Like the player in the picture above, they cannot decide which way to move. Meanwhile, Time forces them into a corner where they can't move.

The great leaders of the world were men and women of quick decision.

General Grant had but little to commend him as an able General except the quality of firm decision, but this was sufficient to offset all of his weaknesses. The whole story of his military success may be gathered from his reply to his critics when he said "We will fight it out along these lines if it takes all summer."

When Napoleon reached a decision to move his armies in a given direction, he permitted nothing to cause him to change that decision. If his line of march brought his soldiers to a ditch, dug by his opponents to stop him, he would give the order to charge the ditch until it had been filled with dead men and horses sufficient to bridge it.

The suspense of indecision drives millions of people to failure. A condemned man once said that the thought of his approaching execution was not so terrifying, once he had reached the decision in his own mind to accept the inevitable.

Lack of decision is the chief stumbling block of all revival meeting workers. Their entire work is to get men and women to reach a decision in their own minds to accept a given religious tenet. Billy Sunday once said, "Indecision is the devil's favorite tool."

Andrew Carnegie visualized a great steel industry, but that industry would not be what it is today had he not reached a decision in his own mind to transform his vision into reality.

James J. Hill saw, in his mind's eye, a great transcontinental railway system, but that railroad never would have become a reality had he not reached a decision to start the project.

Imagination, alone, is not enough to insure success.

Millions of people have imagination and build plans that would easily bring them both fame and fortune, but those plans never reach the DECISION stage.

Walt Disney was a Chicago commercial artist who was clearly on the road to success in his chosen field when he had a vision — and made a decision. He headed west and turned his imagination loose — combined with the firm decision that he was going to create a whole new form of entertainment. The rest is history, millions of Disneyland and Disneyworld visitors will agree.

Demosthenes was a poor Greek lad who had a strong desire to be a great public speaker. Nothing unusual about that; others have "desired" this and similar ability without living to see their desires realized. But, Demosthenes added DECISION to DESIRE, and, despite the fact that he was a stammerer he made himself one of the great orators of the world.

Martin W. Littleton was a poor lad who never saw the inside of a school house until he was past twelve years of age. His father took him to hear a great lawyer defend a murderer, in one of the southern cities. The speech made such a profound impression on the lad's mind that he grabbed his father by the hand and said, "Father, one of these days I am going to become the ablest lawyer in America."

That was a DEFINITE DECISION!

Today Martin W. Littleton accepts no fee under $50,000.00, and it is said that he is kept busy all the time. He became an able lawyer because he reached a DECISION to do so.

Edwin C. Barnes reached a DECISION in his own mind to become the partner of Thomas A. Edison. Handicapped by lack of schooling, without money to pay his railroad fare, and with no influential friends to introduce him to Mr. Edison, young Barnes made his way to East Orange on a freight car and so thoroughly sold himself to Mr. Edison that he got his opportunity which led to a partnership. Today, just twenty years since that decision was reached, Mr. Barnes lives at Bradenton, Florida, retired, with all the money he needs.

Men of decision usually get all that they go after!

Well within the memory of this writer a little group of men met at Westerville, Ohio, and organized what they called the Anti-Saloon League. Saloon men treated them as a joke. People, generally, made fun of them. But, they had reached a decision.

That decision was so pronounced that it finally drove the powerful saloon men into the corner and resulted in Prohibition.

William Wrigley, Jr., reached a decision to devote his entire business career to the manufacture and sale of a five-cent package of chewing gum. His decision brought him financial returns running into millions.

Henry Ford reached a decision to manufacture and sell a popular priced automobile that would be within the means of all who wished to own it. That decision made Ford one of the most powerful men on earth and brought travel opportunity to millions.

All these men had two outstanding qualities: A DEFINITE PUR-
POSE and a firm DECISION to transform that purpose into reality.

The man of DECISION gets that which he goes after, no matter
how long it takes, or how difficult the task. An able salesman wanted
to meet a Cleveland banker. The banker would not see him. One
morning this salesman waited near the banker's house until be saw
him get into his automobile and start downtown. Watching his opportunity, the salesman grove his own automobile into the banker's,
causing slight damage to the automobile. Alighting from his own
car, he handed the banker his card, expressed regret on account of
the damage done, but promised the banker a new car exactly like the
one that had been damaged. That afternoon a new car was delivered
to the banker, and out of that transaction grew a friendship that ter-
minated, finally, in a business partnership which still exists.

The man of DECISION cannot be stopped!

The man of INDECISION cannot be started! Take your own choice.

Behind him lay the gray Azores,
Behind the Gates of Hercules;
Before him not the ghosts of shores;
Before him only shoreless seas.
The good mate said: "Now must we pray,
For lo! the very stars are gone.
Brave Adm'r'l, speak; what shall I say?"
"Why, say: 'Sail on and on!'"

When Columbus began his famous voyage he made one of the
most far-reaching DECISIONS in the history of mankind. Had he not
remained firm on that decision the freedom of America, as we know
it today, would never have been known.

Take notice of those about you and observe this significant fact—THAT THE SUCCESSFUL MEN AND WOMEN ARE THOSE WHO REACH DECISIONS QUICKLY AND THEN STAND FIRMLY BY THOSE DECISIONS AFTER THEY ARE MADE.

If you are one of those who make up their minds today and change them again tomorrow you are doomed to failure. If you are not sure which way to move it is better to shut your eyes and move in the dark than to remain still and make no move at all.

The world will forgive you if you make mistakes, but it will never forgive you if you make no DECISIONS, because it will never hear of you outside of the community in which you live.

No matter who you are or what may be your lifework, you are playing checkers with TIME! It is always your next move. Move with quick DECISION and Time will favor you. Stand still and Time will wipe you off the board.

You cannot always make the right move, but, if you make enough moves you may take advantage of the law of averages and pile up a creditable score before the great game of LIFE is ended.

For more information about Napoleon Hill and available products, please contact the following locations:

Napoleon Hill World Learning Center
Purdue University Calumet
2300 173rd Street
Hammond, Indiana 46323-2094

Judith Williamson, Director
Uriel "Chino" Martinez, Assistant & Graphic Designer

Telephone: 219.989.3173 or 219.989.3166
Email: nhf@purduecal.edu

The Napoleon Hill Foundation
University of Virginia–Wise
College Relations Apt. C
1 College Avenue
Wise, Virginia 24293

Don Green, Executive Director
Annedia Sturgill, Executive Assistant

Telephone: 276.328.6700
Email: napoleonhill@uvawise.edu

Website: www.naphill.org

Made in the USA
San Bernardino, CA
26 April 2020